W9-CBB-074

**BART SIMPSON BLASTOFF**

Materials previously published in
Bart Simpson #55, 59-62

FIRST EDITION

ISBN 978-0-06-236061-8

15 16 17 18 19 TC 10 9 8 7 6 5 4 3 2 1

Publisher: Matt Groening
Creative Director: Nathan Kane
Managing Editor: Terry Delegeane
Director of Operations: Robert Zaugh
Art Director: Jason Ho
Art Director Special Projects: Serban Cristescu
Assistant Art Director: Mike Rote
Production Manager: Christopher Ungar
Assistant Editor: Karen Bates
Production: Art Villanueva
Administration: Ruth Waytz, Pete Benson
Legal Guardian: Susan A. Grode

Printed by TC Transcontinental, Beauceville, QC, Canada. 02/20/2015

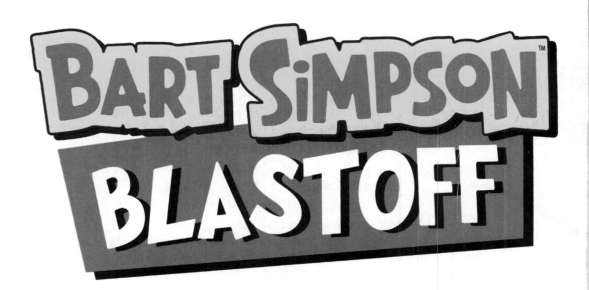

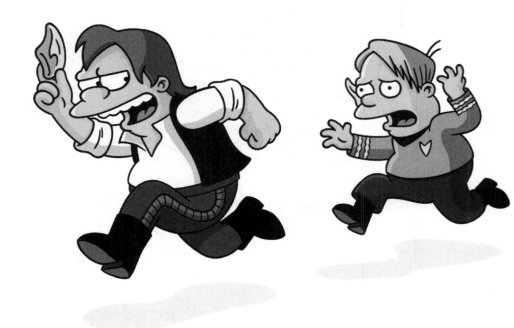

# HARPER

NEW YORK • LONDON • TORONTO • SYDNEY

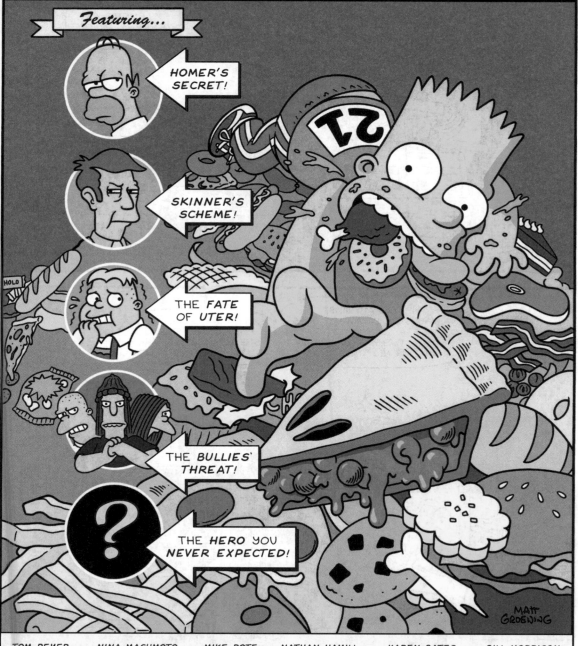

# BART SIMPSON in
# EAT THE PIE SLOWLY

Featuring...

HOMER'S SECRET!

SKINNER'S SCHEME!

THE *FATE* OF *UTER!*

THE *BULLIES'* THREAT!

**?**

THE *HERO* YOU NEVER EXPECTED!

MATT GROENING

TOM PEYER
SCRIPT

NINA MASUMOTO
PENCILS

MIKE ROTE
INKS

NATHAN HAMILL
COLORS

KAREN BATES
LETTERS

BILL MORRISON
EDITOR

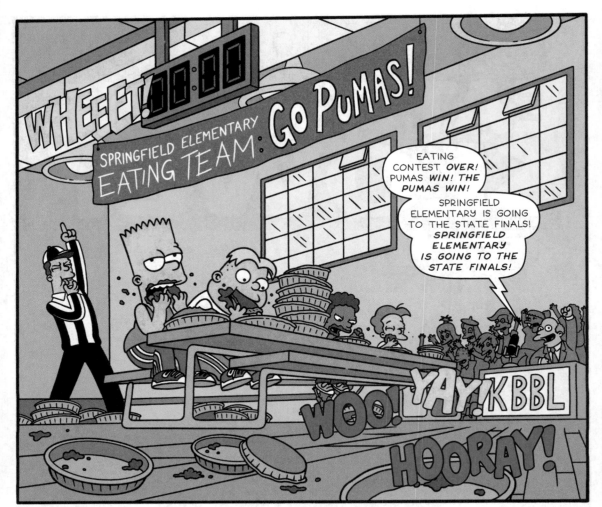

WHEEET! 00:00

SPRINGFIELD ELEMENTARY EATING TEAM: GO PUMAS!

EATING CONTEST *OVER*! PUMAS *WIN*! *THE PUMAS WIN*! SPRINGFIELD ELEMENTARY IS GOING TO THE STATE FINALS! *SPRINGFIELD ELEMENTARY IS GOING TO THE STATE FINALS!*

WOO! YAY! KBBL

HOORAY!

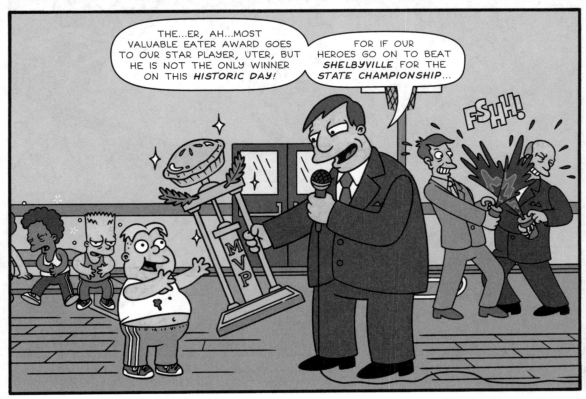

THE...ER, AH...MOST VALUABLE EATER AWARD GOES TO OUR STAR PLAYER, UTER, BUT HE IS NOT THE ONLY WINNER ON THIS *HISTORIC DAY*!

FOR IF OUR HEROES GO ON TO BEAT *SHELBYVILLE* FOR THE *STATE CHAMPIONSHIP*...

FSHH!

MVP

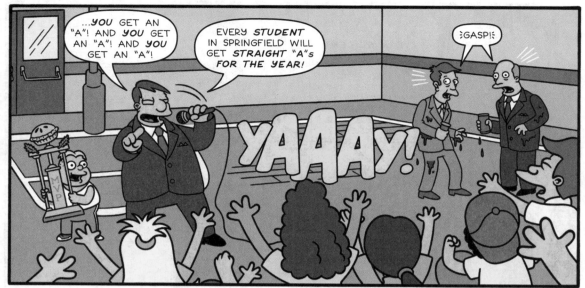

...*YOU* GET AN "A"! AND *YOU* GET AN "A"! AND *YOU* GET AN "A"!

EVERY *STUDENT* IN SPRINGFIELD WILL GET *STRAIGHT* "A"s *FOR THE YEAR!*

⸮GASP!⸝

YAAAY!

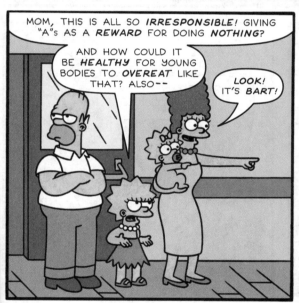

MOM, THIS IS ALL SO *IRRESPONSIBLE!* GIVING "A"s AS A *REWARD* FOR DOING *NOTHING?*

AND HOW COULD IT BE *HEALTHY* FOR YOUNG BODIES TO *OVEREAT* LIKE THAT? ALSO--

*LOOK!* IT'S *BART!*

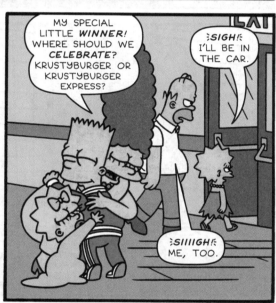

MY SPECIAL LITTLE *WINNER!* WHERE SHOULD WE *CELEBRATE?* KRUSTYBURGER OR KRUSTYBURGER EXPRESS?

⸮SIGH⸝ I'LL BE IN THE CAR.

⸮SIIIIGH⸝ ME, TOO.

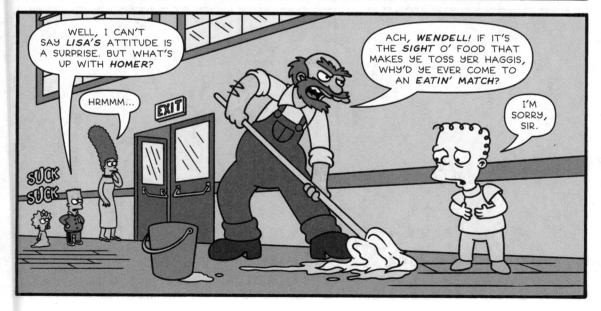

WELL, I CAN'T SAY *LISA'S* ATTITUDE IS A SURPRISE. BUT WHAT'S UP WITH *HOMER?*

HRMMM...

ACH, *WENDELL!* IF IT'S THE *SIGHT* O' FOOD THAT MAKES YE TOSS YER *HAGGIS,* WHY'D YE EVER COME TO AN *EATIN' MATCH?*

I'M SORRY, SIR.

SUCK SUCK

EXIT

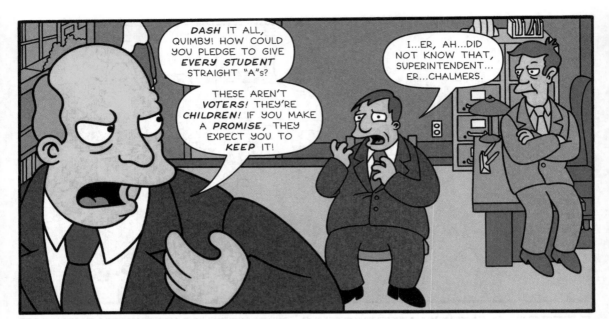

DASH IT ALL, QUIMBY! HOW COULD YOU PLEDGE TO GIVE *EVERY STUDENT* STRAIGHT "A"s?

THESE AREN'T *VOTERS!* THEY'RE *CHILDREN!* IF YOU MAKE A *PROMISE,* THEY EXPECT YOU TO *KEEP* IT!

I...ER, AH...DID NOT KNOW THAT, SUPERINTENDENT... ER...CHALMERS.

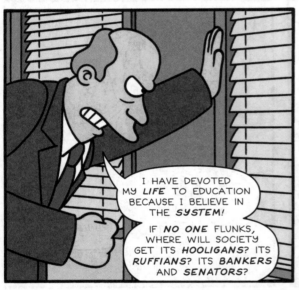

I HAVE DEVOTED MY *LIFE* TO EDUCATION BECAUSE I BELIEVE IN THE *SYSTEM!*

IF *NO ONE* FLUNKS, WHERE WILL SOCIETY GET ITS *HOOLIGANS?* ITS *RUFFIANS?* ITS *BANKERS* AND *SENATORS?*

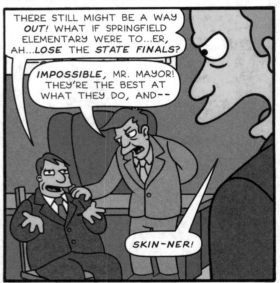

THERE STILL MIGHT BE A WAY *OUT!* WHAT IF SPRINGFIELD ELEMENTARY WERE TO...ER, AH...*LOSE* THE *STATE FINALS?*

*IMPOSSIBLE,* MR. MAYOR! THEY'RE THE BEST AT WHAT THEY DO, AND--

SKIN-NER!

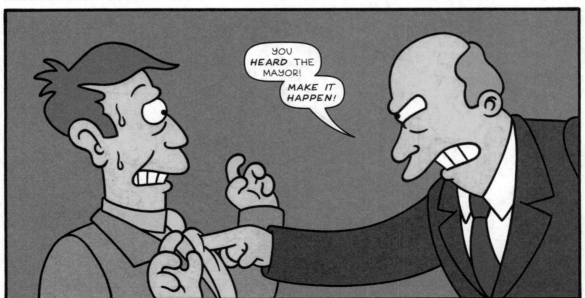

YOU *HEARD* THE MAYOR!

*MAKE IT HAPPEN!*

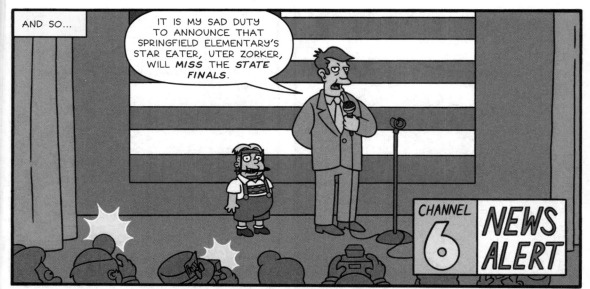

AND SO...

IT IS MY SAD DUTY TO ANNOUNCE THAT SPRINGFIELD ELEMENTARY'S STAR EATER, UTER ZORKER, WILL *MISS* THE *STATE FINALS*.

CHANNEL **6** **NEWS ALERT**

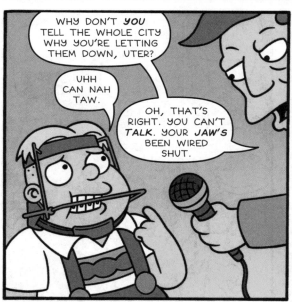

WHY DON'T *YOU* TELL THE WHOLE CITY WHY YOU'RE LETTING THEM DOWN, UTER?

UHH CAN NAH TAW.

OH, THAT'S RIGHT. YOU CAN'T *TALK*. YOUR *JAW'S* BEEN WIRED SHUT.

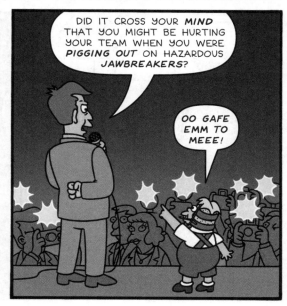

DID IT CROSS YOUR *MIND* THAT YOU MIGHT BE HURTING YOUR TEAM WHEN YOU WERE *PIGGING OUT* ON HAZARDOUS *JAWBREAKERS*?

OO GAFE EMM TO MEEE!

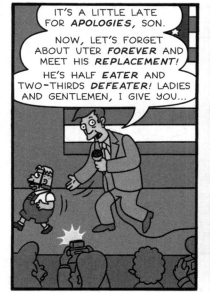

IT'S A LITTLE LATE FOR *APOLOGIES*, SON.

NOW, LET'S FORGET ABOUT UTER *FOREVER* AND MEET HIS *REPLACEMENT!*

HE'S HALF *EATER* AND TWO-THIRDS *DEFEATER!* LADIES AND GENTLEMEN, I GIVE YOU...

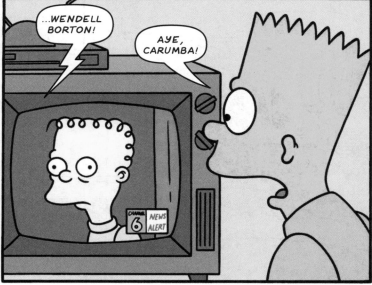

...WENDELL BORTON!

AYE, CARUMBA!

CHANNEL 6 NEWS ALERT

DAD, WE'RE DOOMED! WENDELL CAN'T EVEN KEEP DOWN STOMACH MEDICINE. SHELBYVILLE'S GONNA KILL US.
AND MAYBE THAT'LL END THIS "COMPETITIVE EATING" NONSENSE ONCE AND FOR ALL!
GROAN
WHERE ARE YOU GOING? YOU'RE NOT EATING, ARE YOU?
DON'T LET ME CATCH YOU EATING!
BART! WE HEARD ABOUT UTER!
YOU'D BETTER CARRY THE TEAM NOW!
YEAH! MAYOR QUIMBY'S PROMISE GAVE US DREAMS FOR THE FUTURE! WHEN I GROW UP...
...I'M GOING TO BE AN ACTUARY!
I'M GOING TO BE A COMPTROLLER!
I'M GOING TO BE AN OMBUDSMAN!
SO GET US THOSE STRAIGHT "A"s...
...OR ELSE!
YEAH! OR ELSE!
HRMMM...

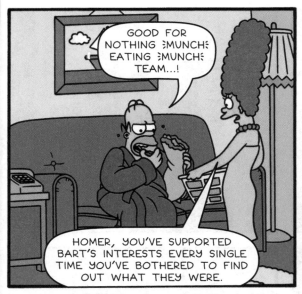

GOOD FOR NOTHING :MUNCH: EATING :MUNCH: TEAM...!

HOMER, YOU'VE SUPPORTED BART'S INTERESTS EVERY SINGLE TIME YOU'VE BOTHERED TO FIND OUT WHAT THEY WERE.

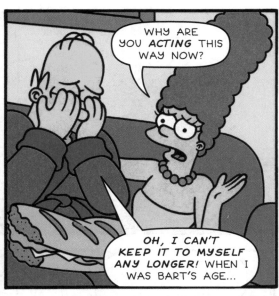

WHY ARE YOU *ACTING* THIS WAY NOW?

OH, I CAN'T *KEEP IT TO MYSELF ANY LONGER!* WHEN I WAS BART'S AGE...

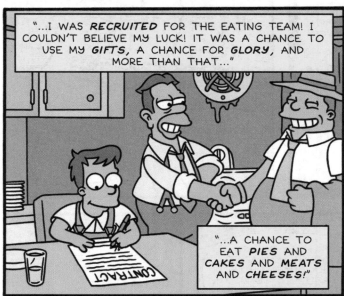

"...I WAS *RECRUITED* FOR THE EATING TEAM! I COULDN'T BELIEVE MY LUCK! IT WAS A CHANCE TO USE MY *GIFTS,* A CHANCE FOR *GLORY,* AND MORE THAN THAT..."

"...A CHANCE TO EAT *PIES* AND *CAKES* AND *MEATS* AND *CHEESES!*"

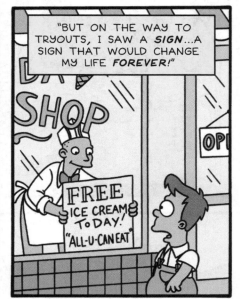

"BUT ON THE WAY TO TRYOUTS, I SAW A *SIGN*...A SIGN THAT WOULD CHANGE MY LIFE *FOREVER!*"

SHOP

OP

FREE ICE CREAM TODAY! "ALL-U-CAN EAT"

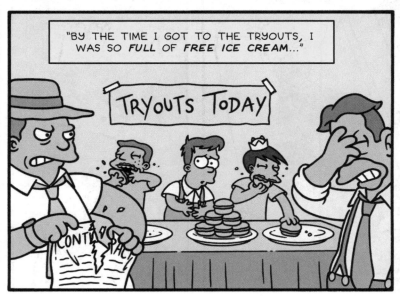

"BY THE TIME I GOT TO THE TRYOUTS, I WAS SO *FULL* OF *FREE ICE CREAM*..."

TRYOUTS TODAY

CONTRACT

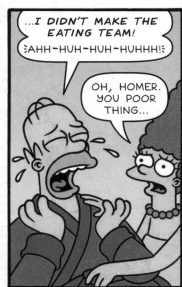

...I DIDN'T MAKE THE EATING TEAM! :AHH-HUH-HUH-HUHHH!:

OH, HOMER. YOU POOR THING...

HOMER, I KNOW THESE MEMORIES ARE PAINFUL, BUT THEY'RE NOT BART'S FAULT!

ʒSNIFF!!ʒ

ALL THIS *EATING* IS EATING HIM *UP*. HE NEEDS A FATHER'S *GUIDANCE*. IF YOU CAN GIVE YOUR LITTLE BOY *THAT*...

...YOU'LL FINALLY BE THE EATING CHAMPION YOU ALWAYS KNEW YOU COULD BE.

NO I WON'T.

WELL, IN A WAY.

I DON'T SEE HOW. BUT, HEY, I'LL GIVE IT A SHOT.

FIRST, I'LL TRASH ALL MY HIDDEN CANDY... THEN I'LL QUIT THE TEAM...AND THEN...

BART! COME DOWN FOR DINNER!

NO! I'M *NEVER EATING FOOD AGAIN!*

THERE IS MUCH *ANGER* IN YOU.

WHAT THE--?!

YOU MUST UNLEARN ALL YOU HAVE LEARNED. THE HOUR HAS COME FOR THE MASTER TO TEACH THE APPRENTICE *THE WAY OF THE FOOD*.

*REALLY*, DAD?

CONTROL *MUNCH* CONTROL *SMACK*...YOU MUST LEARN *CHOMP* **CONTROL**.
12:15 AM
CHIPS
KRUSTY O's
NO, NO, **NO**. YOU MUST FEEL **THE FOOD** AROUND YOU.
**THE FOOD** IS YOUR ALLY. AND A POWERFUL ALLY IT IS. LIFE CREATES IT, MAKES IT GROW. ITS TASTE SURROUNDS AND BINDS US.
CHOMP!
MUNCH!
I SEE YOU ARE BEGINNING TO **UNDERSTAND**.
11:27 AM
**THE FOOD** IS STRONG IN YOUR FAMILY. PASS ON WHAT YOU HAVE LEARNED.
NOW, WHEN'S THIS **EATING CONTEST**, ANYWAY?
11:50
IT'S...
OH, **NO!** IT'S IN **TEN MINUTES!** AND I'M ALL FULL UP!
AWWW...
...YOU'RE A BIG DISAPPOINTMENT, JUST LIKE YOUR OL' DAD.

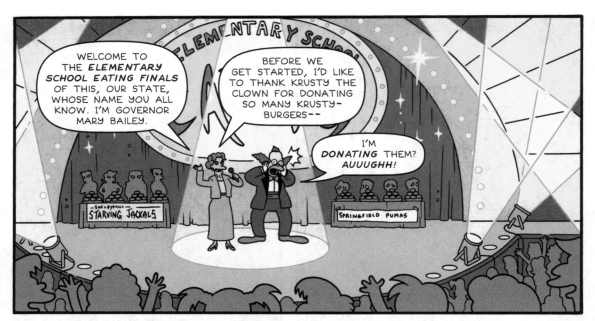

WELCOME TO THE *ELEMENTARY SCHOOL EATING FINALS* OF THIS, OUR STATE, WHOSE NAME YOU ALL KNOW. I'M GOVERNOR MARY BAILEY.

BEFORE WE GET STARTED, I'D LIKE TO THANK KRUSTY THE CLOWN FOR DONATING SO MANY KRUSTY-BURGERS--

I'M *DONATING* THEM? AUUUGHH!

STARVING JACKALS

SPRINGFIELD PUMAS

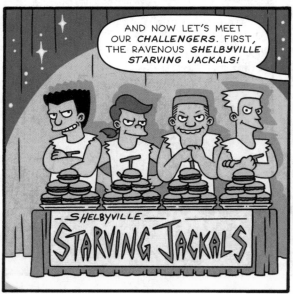

AND NOW LET'S MEET OUR *CHALLENGERS*. FIRST, THE RAVENOUS *SHELBYVILLE STARVING JACKALS!*

— SHELBYVILLE —
STARVING JACKALS

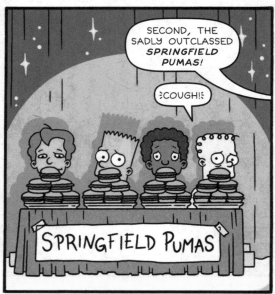

SECOND, THE SADLY OUTCLASSED *SPRINGFIELD PUMAS!*

⸬COUGH!⸬

SPRINGFIELD PUMAS

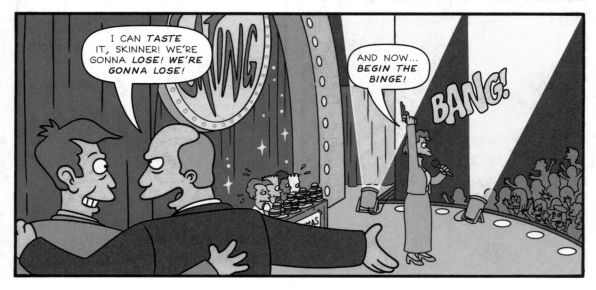

I CAN *TASTE* IT, SKINNER! WE'RE GONNA *LOSE!* WE'RE GONNA LOSE!

AND NOW... *BEGIN THE BINGE!*

BANG!

GUUUH!
AAH!
HEH, HEH!
YOU CAN DO IT, BOY!
FOOD
GROAN
TWEET!
THE CONTEST IS OVER AND OUR NEW STATE CHAMPION EATING TEAM IS...

...THE SPRINGFIELD PUMAS!
WENDELL! YOU ATE ALL THAT? BUT HOW?
EH, MIGHT AS WELL. I'LL BE SICK EITHER WAY...
FIRST PLACE
SHELBYVILLE
STARVING JACKALS
SKIN-NER! ANY MORE BRIGHT IDEAS?
I'LL THINK OF ONE, SIR! I SWEAR!
THREE MONTHS LATER...
YAAAY!
STRAIGHT "A"s! OMBUDSMAN SCHOOL HERE I COME!
I GOT... STRAIGHT ASTERISKS?
El Barto
REPORT
DON'T TELL ANYONE, LISA! IT'S OUR NEW GRADING SYSTEM. ASTERISKS REPLACE "A"s AND "A" IS THE NEW "D."
REPORT
SIMPSON, LISA
Reading *
Writing *
Arithmetic *
Sitting Still *
Folding hands on desk *
ALL "A"s? LET'S CELEBRATE, BOY!
LAST ONE FINISHED IS A BIG, FAT LOSER!
THAT'LL BE YOU!
NO YOU.
NO, YOU.
KRUSTY BURGER
NO, GLUUUHH
MUGGHH-UGGGH GULP!
THE END

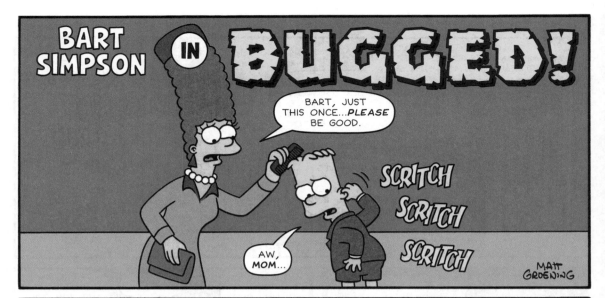

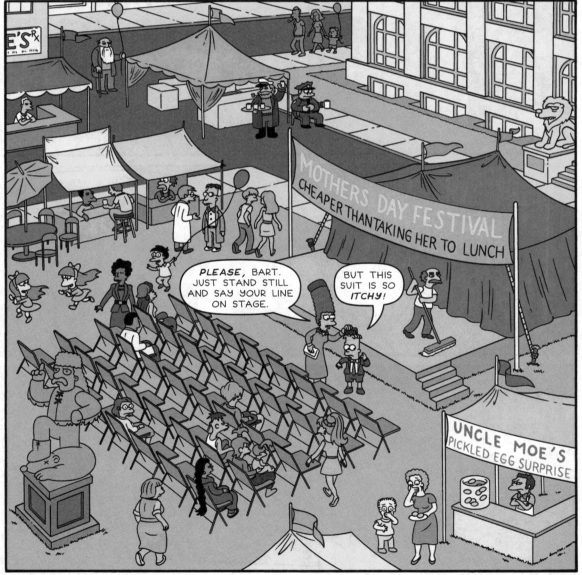

DAVID SEIDMAN
SCRIPT

DEXTER REED
PENCILS

MIKE ROTE
INKS

NATHAN HAMILL
COLORS

KAREN BATES
LETTERS

BILL MORRISON
EDITOR

HELLO, MARGE! I SEE YOUR BART AND MY JESSICA ARE IN THE "TRIBUTE TO MOTHERS" SHOW.
I HOPE BART DOESN'T **EMBARRASS** YOU THE WAY HE DID AT THE EASTER PAGEANT. HOW **DID** HE GET A ROTARY SPRINKLER FULL OF FAKE BLOOD INTO THE CRUCIFIXION SCENE?
IF HE MISBEHAVES TODAY, I'M SURE YOU'LL NEVER HEAR THE **END** OF IT!
SCRITCH
SCRITCH
SCRITCH
SEE WHAT I HAVE TO PUT UP WITH?
I'LL BE GOOD.
"M STANDS FOR..."...HOW'S MY LINE END AGAIN?
"MOTHER."
PRINCIPAL SKINNER? WHAT ARE **YOU** DOING IN THE SHOW?
MOTHER INSISTED. SHE WAS RIGHT, OF COURSE.
SOMEONE'S MAKING YOU LOOK LIKE A DORK? I LIKE HER ALREADY.
STAGE MANAGER
PLACES, PEOPLE! YOU'RE **ON**!
STAGE MANAGER

HEY! WATCH IT WITH THE SODA!
HOPE IT DOESN'T ATTRACT ANTS. THEY'D MAKE YOU SCRATCH LIKE A WILD MONKEY!
SPLUSH
THAT'D BE SO EMBARRASSING TO YOUR MOMMY!
AND NOW, FOR ALL YOU MOMS OUT THERE...
*
*IF THIS KID'S GOT SWEET STUFF ON HIS SHOES, HE'S GOTTA HAVE IT ELSEWHERE. ANTS...FOLLOW ME UP HIS BODY!
...A TRIBUTE TO MOTHERS!
DON'T SCRATCH. DON'T SCRATCH. DON'T SCRATCH.
"M" STANDS FOR...UH... MOTHER.
GOTTA SCRATCH!
"O" STANDS FOR...
...THE OBEDIENCE WE OWE HER.
"T" STANDS FOR...

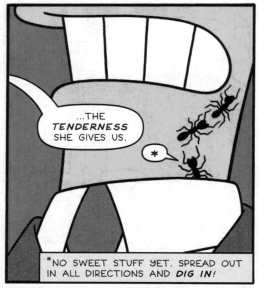

...THE *TENDERNESS* SHE GIVES US.

\*

\*NO SWEET STUFF YET. SPREAD OUT IN ALL DIRECTIONS AND *DIG IN!*

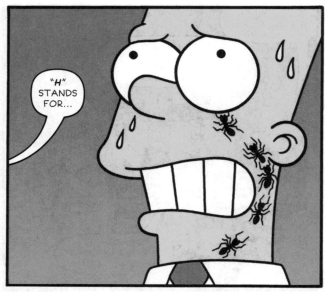

*"H"* STANDS FOR...

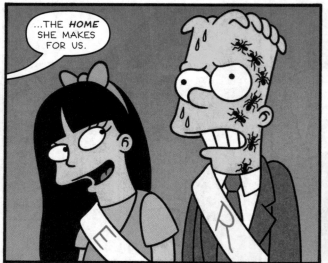

...THE *HOME* SHE MAKES FOR US.

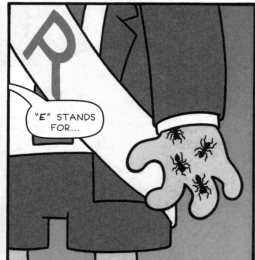

*"E"* STANDS FOR...

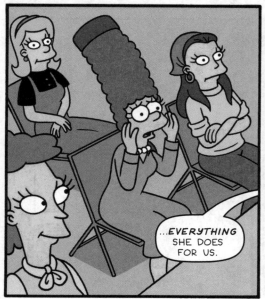

...*EVERYTHING* SHE DOES FOR US.

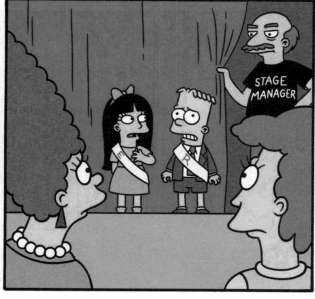

STAGE MANAGER

"R" STANDS FOR THE RESPECT SHE DESERVES!
STAGE MANAGER
WHEW!
HMPH!
HAPPY MOTHER'S DAY!
WELL, MARGE, I HAVE TO HAND IT TO YOU. BART WAS A PERFECT GENTLEMAN. WE MAY AS WELL GO BACKSTAGE AND CONGRATULATE HIM.
THANKS, HELEN.
I THINK BART'S REALLY STARTING TO MATURE!
#@$&!!
SCRATCH!
SCRATCH!
SCRATCH!
THE END

# MAGGIE'S CRIB

by ARAGONÉS

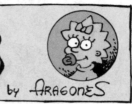

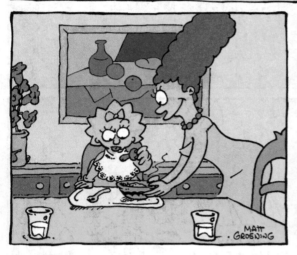

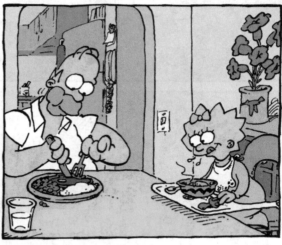

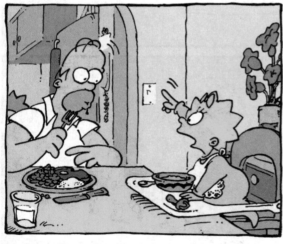

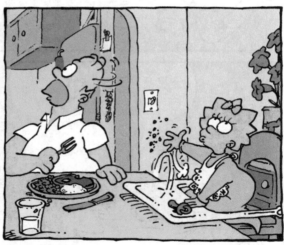

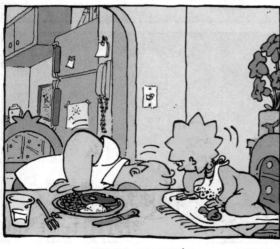

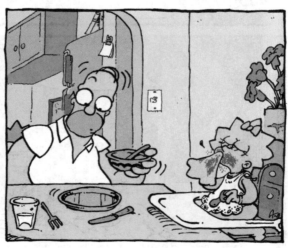

**SERGIO ARAGONÉS**
STORY & ART

**ART VILLANUEVA**
COLORS

**BILL MORRISON**
EDITOR

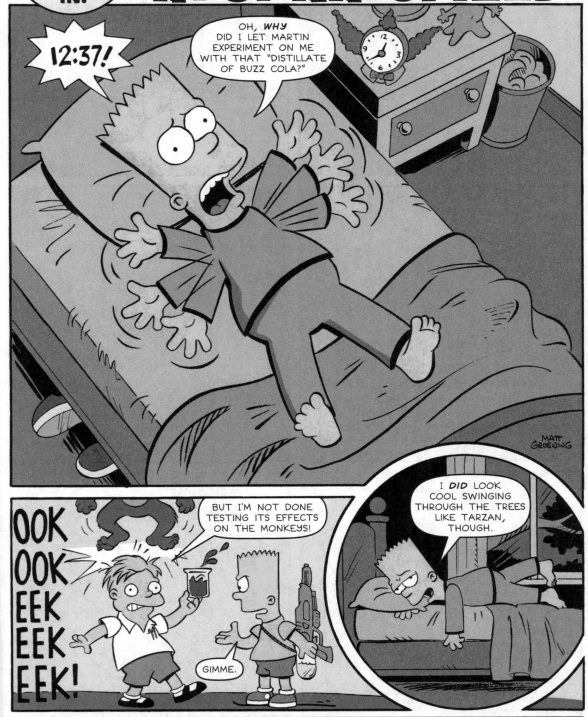

# BART & MAGGIE SIMPSON IN: SLEEPLESS IN SPRINGFIELD

12:37!

OH, *WHY* DID I LET MARTIN EXPERIMENT ON ME WITH THAT "DISTILLATE OF BUZZ COLA?"

MATT GROENING

BUT I'M NOT DONE TESTING ITS EFFECTS ON THE MONKEYS!

OOK OOK EEK EEK EEK!

GIMME.

I *DID* LOOK COOL SWINGING THROUGH THE TREES LIKE TARZAN, THOUGH.

CAROL LAY
STORY & ART

NATHAN HAMILL
COLORS

KAREN BATES
LETTERS

BILL MORRISON
EDITOR

USUALLY I CAN SLEEP LIKE A BEAR ANYTIME I WANT. EXCEPT CHRISTMAS EVE, OF COURSE.
SOMEDAY I'LL CATCH THAT RED-SUITED OLD FAT GUY IN THE ACT, YESSIR.
USUALLY I CAN EVEN SLEEP THROUGH HOMER'S SNORING.
ZZZZZZZZZZ
NOT TONIGHT, THOUGH. I WONDER IF EARPLUGS WILL DO THE TRICK.
HERE THEY ARE...SAXOPHONE PROTECTION JOBBIES!
YUK! MAYBE I SHOULDN'T HAVE USED THEM AS EYEBALLS ON MY MUD MONSTER...
GREAT. NOW LISA IS SINGING IN HER SLEEP AGAIN.
I NEVER DID LIKE VHAHG-NER...
MAYBE THE TREE HOUSE WILL BE QUIETER THAN THIS ZOO.
ZZZZZZ

ARF ARF!
CREEAK
THUMP
NOPE. NOT QUIETER.
RADIOACTIVE MAN
ARF! ARF!
I WONDER IF IT'S TOO LATE TO CALL MILHOUSE TO SEE IF I CAN SLEEP OVER?
RINNG RINNG
RINNG RINNG
Z Z Z Z Z Z Z Z
APPARENTLY, MARTIN DID NOT FORCE HIS POISONOUS POTION ON MY GOOD BUDDY MILHOUSE, LUCKY DEVIL.
IF I'M GOING TO BE UP ALL NIGHT I MIGHT AS WELL GET IN SOME VIEWING. I WONDER WHAT'S ON?
KLICK!

MAGSTER! DID I WAKE YOU UP? OR DID MARTIN GET TO YOU, TOO, WITH THAT NOXIOUS BREW?
SUCK SUCK
IT'S TIME TO EDUCATE YOU ON THE JOYS OF LATE-NIGHT TELEVISION!
CLICK!
COOL! "MCBAIN MEETS THE BRAIN!" MOM THINKS IT'S TOO VIOLENT FOR KIDS.
WE'LL JUST SEE ABOUT THAT.
SUCK SUCK
I HEAR IT'S SO VIOLENT, THEY'LL ONLY RUN IT ON TV IN THE WEE HOURS.
THIS, YOUNG MISS, IS A WEE HOUR.
NO, NOT THAT KIND OF "WEE."
OH, OKAY.

FLUSSHHHHhhh...
KA-BLOOOIE!
NUTS! WE JUST MISSED A MAJOR EXPLOSION. NOW WE'LL GET LIKE AN HOUR OF COMMERCIALS.
CAN'T SLEEP? CAN'T COUNT ON COUNTING SHEEP?
WEIRD. IT'S LIKE THE TV IS READING MY MIND!
SUCK SUCK
TRY INSOMNIAX, THE SLEEP AID THAT AIDS SLEEP!
AVAILABLE AT PHARMACIES EVERYWHERE.
NEW!
Insomniax
THAT'S IT! I'LL WAKE UP HOMER AND MAKE HIM DRIVE ME TO THE PHARMACY!

OH. THE PHARMACY'S CLOSED.
I'LL NEVER GET TO SLEEP.
AND TOMORROW'S A SCHOOL DAY. I HAVE TO GET UP SOON.
THUP!
SUCK SUCK
YOU WANT ME TO READ YOU A STORY? OKAY!
HOW ABOUT THIS ONE, THE VELVETEEN RABBIT?

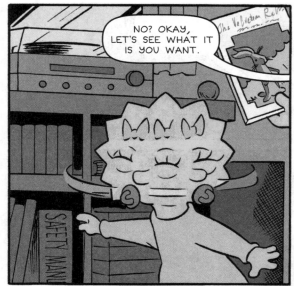

NO? OKAY, LET'S SEE WHAT IT IS YOU WANT.

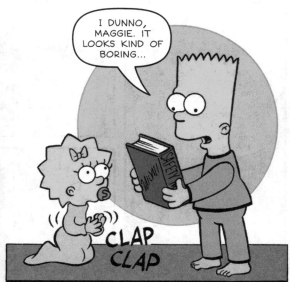

I DUNNO, MAGGIE. IT LOOKS KIND OF BORING...

CLAP CLAP

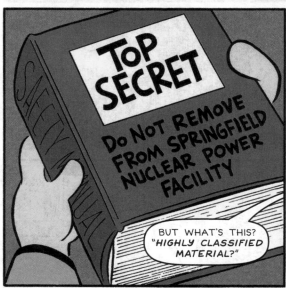

BUT WHAT'S THIS? "HIGHLY CLASSIFIED MATERIAL?"

TOP SECRET

Do Not REMOVE FROM SPRINGFIELD NUCLEAR POWER FACILITY

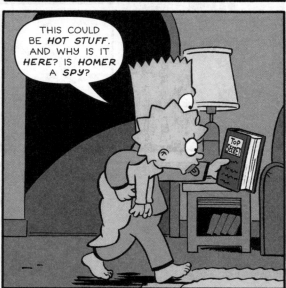

THIS COULD BE HOT STUFF. AND WHY IS IT HERE? IS HOMER A SPY?

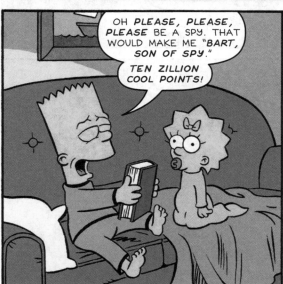

OH PLEASE, PLEASE, PLEASE BE A SPY. THAT WOULD MAKE ME "BART, SON OF SPY."

TEN ZILLION COOL POINTS!

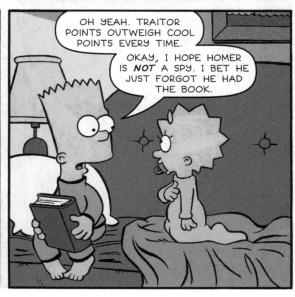

OH YEAH. TRAITOR POINTS OUTWEIGH COOL POINTS EVERY TIME.

OKAY, I HOPE HOMER IS NOT A SPY. I BET HE JUST FORGOT HE HAD THE BOOK.

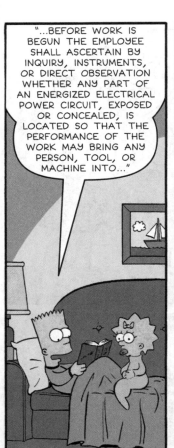

"...BEFORE WORK IS BEGUN THE EMPLOYEE SHALL ASCERTAIN BY INQUIRY, INSTRUMENTS, OR DIRECT OBSERVATION WHETHER ANY PART OF AN ENERGIZED ELECTRICAL POWER CIRCUIT, EXPOSED OR CONCEALED, IS LOCATED SO THAT THE PERFORMANCE OF THE WORK MAY BRING ANY PERSON, TOOL, OR MACHINE INTO..."

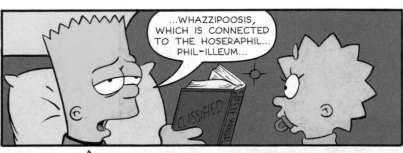

...WHAZZIPOOSIS, WHICH IS CONNECTED TO THE HOSERAPHIL... PHIL-ILLEUM...

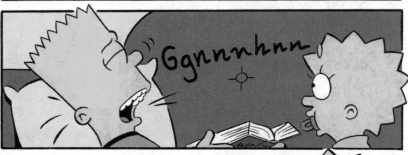

Ggnnnhnn

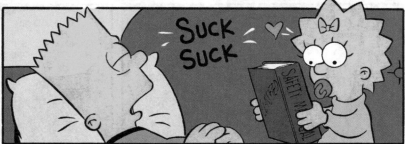

Suck Suck

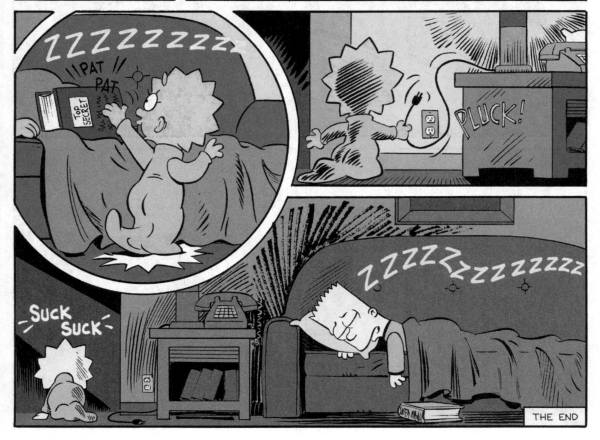

ZZZZZZZZZ

PAT PAT

TOP SECRET

PLUCK!

ZZZZZZzzzzzzzz

SUCK SUCK

THE END

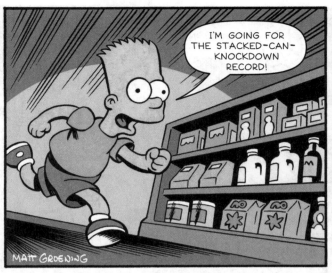

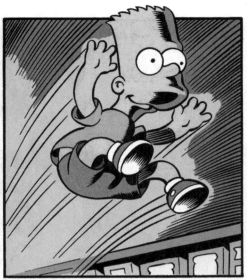

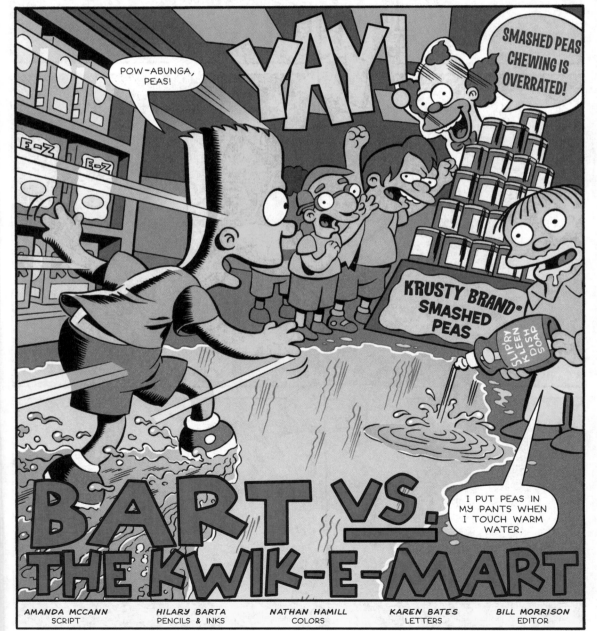

AMANDA McCANN
SCRIPT

HILARY BARTA
PENCILS & INKS

NATHAN HAMILL
COLORS

KAREN BATES
LETTERS

BILL MORRISON
EDITOR

STOP, IN THE NAME OF ALL THAT IS WHOLESALE!
BART SIMPSON, I SAID "STOP!"
APU, MOVE OUT OF THE WAY! I CAN'T!
CRASH!
NEW!
NEW!
YOU ARE IN A WORLD OF TROUBLE, MR. BART.
UH-OH.
SALE

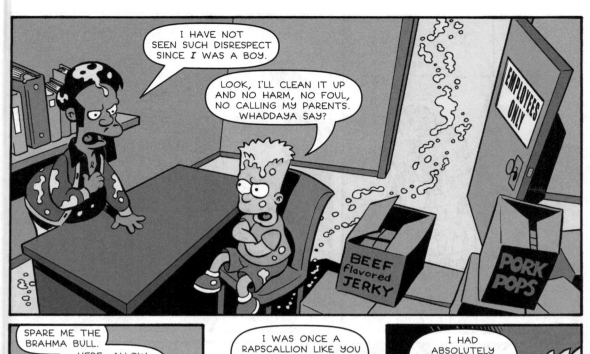

I HAVE NOT SEEN SUCH DISRESPECT SINCE *I* WAS A BOY.

LOOK, I'LL CLEAN IT UP AND NO HARM, NO FOUL, NO CALLING MY PARENTS. WHADDAYA SAY?

EMPLOYEES ONLY

BEEF flavored JERKY

PORK POPS

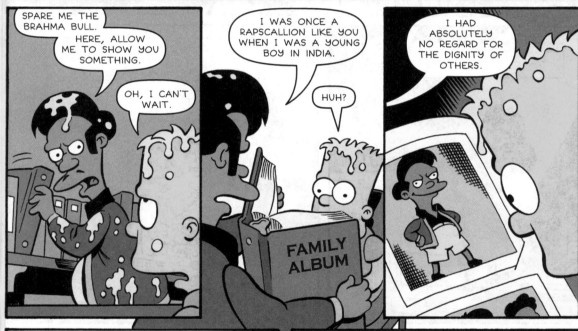

SPARE ME THE BRAHMA BULL. HERE, ALLOW ME TO SHOW YOU SOMETHING.

OH, I CAN'T WAIT.

I WAS ONCE A RAPSCALLION LIKE YOU WHEN I WAS A YOUNG BOY IN INDIA.

HUH?

I HAD ABSOLUTELY NO REGARD FOR THE DIGNITY OF OTHERS.

FAMILY ALBUM

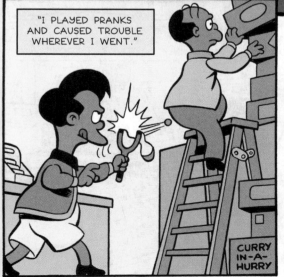

"I PLAYED PRANKS AND CAUSED TROUBLE WHEREVER I WENT."

CURRY IN-A-HURRY

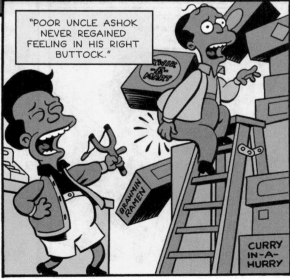

"POOR UNCLE ASHOK NEVER REGAINED FEELING IN HIS RIGHT BUTTOCK."

BRAHMIN RAMEN

CURRY IN-A-HURRY

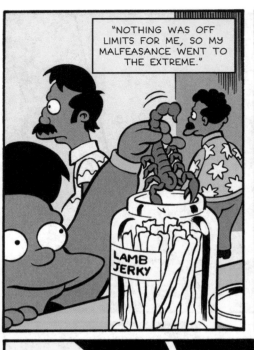

"NOTHING WAS OFF LIMITS FOR ME, SO MY MALFEASANCE WENT TO THE EXTREME."

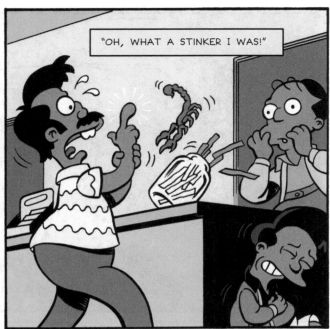

"OH, WHAT A STINKER I WAS!"

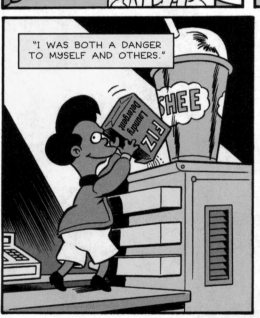

"I WAS BOTH A DANGER TO MYSELF AND OTHERS."

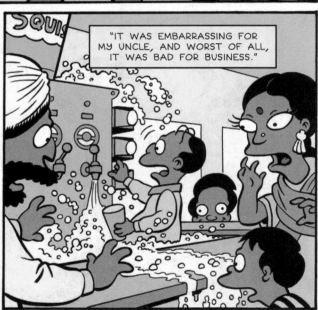

"IT WAS EMBARRASSING FOR MY UNCLE, AND WORST OF ALL, IT WAS BAD FOR BUSINESS."

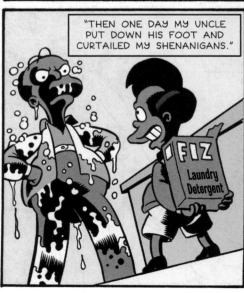

"THEN ONE DAY MY UNCLE PUT DOWN HIS FOOT AND CURTAILED MY SHENANIGANS."

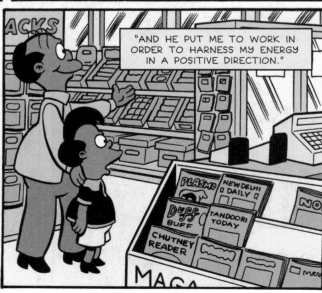

"AND HE PUT ME TO WORK IN ORDER TO HARNESS MY ENERGY IN A POSITIVE DIRECTION."

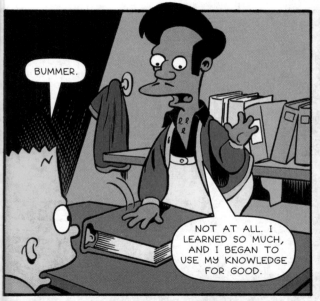

BUMMER.

NOT AT ALL. I LEARNED SO MUCH, AND I BEGAN TO USE MY KNOWLEDGE FOR GOOD.

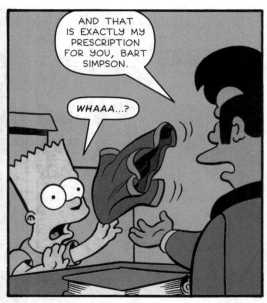

AND THAT IS EXACTLY MY PRESCRIPTION FOR YOU, BART SIMPSON.

WHAAA...?

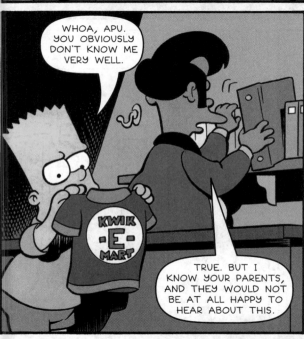

WHOA, APU. YOU OBVIOUSLY DON'T KNOW ME VERY WELL.

TRUE. BUT I KNOW YOUR PARENTS, AND THEY WOULD NOT BE AT ALL HAPPY TO HEAR ABOUT THIS.

KWIK ·E· MART

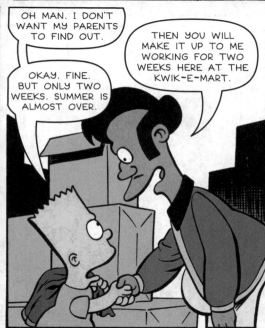

OH MAN. I DON'T WANT MY PARENTS TO FIND OUT.

OKAY. FINE. BUT ONLY TWO WEEKS. SUMMER IS ALMOST OVER.

THEN YOU WILL MAKE IT UP TO ME WORKING FOR TWO WEEKS HERE AT THE KWIK-E-MART.

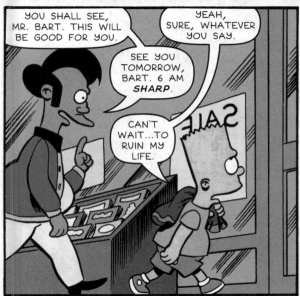

YOU SHALL SEE, MR. BART. THIS WILL BE GOOD FOR YOU.

SEE YOU TOMORROW, BART. 6 AM *SHARP*.

YEAH, SURE, WHATEVER YOU SAY.

CAN'T WAIT...TO RUIN MY LIFE.

SALE

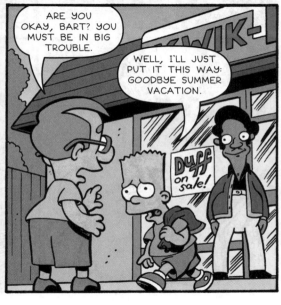

ARE YOU OKAY, BART? YOU MUST BE IN BIG TROUBLE.

WELL, I'LL JUST PUT IT THIS WAY: GOODBYE SUMMER VACATION.

Duff on sale!

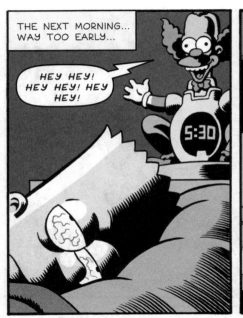

THE NEXT MORNING... WAY TOO EARLY...

HEY HEY! HEY HEY! HEY HEY!

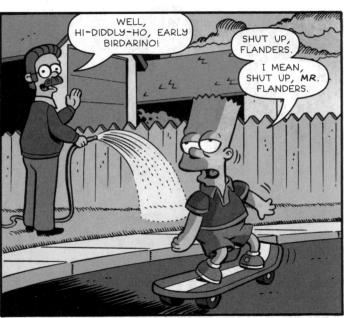

WELL, HI-DIDDLY-HO, EARLY BIRDARINO!

SHUT UP, FLANDERS. I MEAN, SHUT UP, MR. FLANDERS.

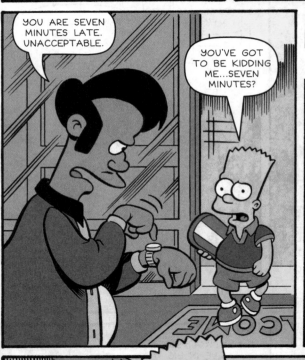

YOU ARE SEVEN MINUTES LATE. UNACCEPTABLE.

YOU'VE GOT TO BE KIDDING ME...SEVEN MINUTES?

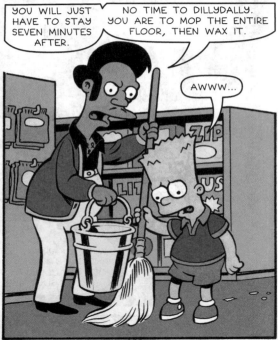

YOU WILL JUST HAVE TO STAY SEVEN MINUTES AFTER.

NO TIME TO DILLYDALLY. YOU ARE TO MOP THE ENTIRE FLOOR, THEN WAX IT.

AWWW...

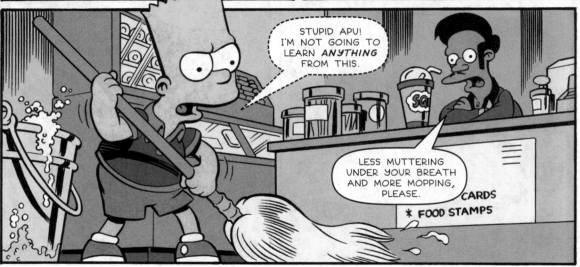

STUPID APU! I'M NOT GOING TO LEARN ANYTHING FROM THIS.

LESS MUTTERING UNDER YOUR BREATH AND MORE MOPPING, PLEASE.

CARDS

* FOOD STAMPS

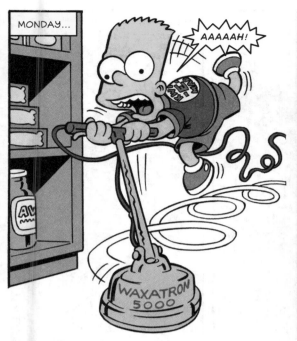

MONDAY...

AAAAAH!

WAXATRON 5000

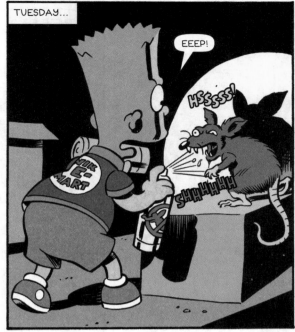

TUESDAY...

EEEP!

HSSSSS!

SHHHHH

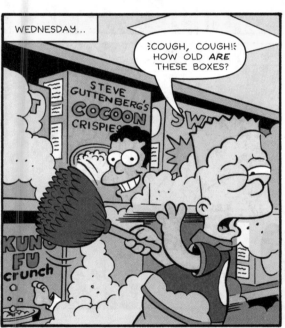

WEDNESDAY...

:COUGH, COUGH!: HOW OLD *ARE* THESE BOXES?

STEVE GUTTENBERG'S COCOON CRISPIES

KUNG FU crunch

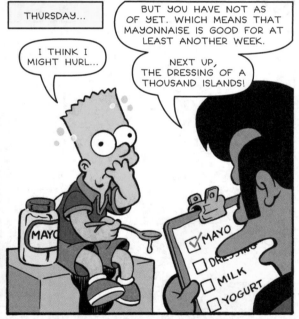

THURSDAY...

BUT YOU HAVE NOT AS OF YET. WHICH MEANS THAT MAYONNAISE IS GOOD FOR AT LEAST ANOTHER WEEK.

NEXT UP, THE DRESSING OF A THOUSAND ISLANDS!

I THINK I MIGHT HURL...

MAYO

☑ MAYO
☐ DRESSING
☐ MILK
☐ YOGURT

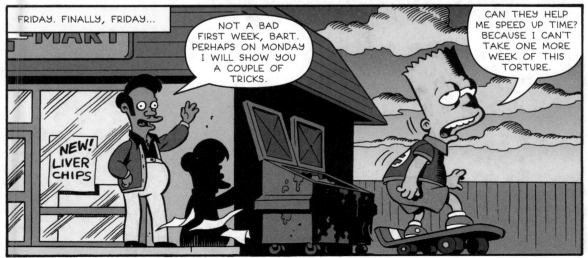

FRIDAY. FINALLY, FRIDAY...

NOT A BAD FIRST WEEK, BART. PERHAPS ON MONDAY I WILL SHOW YOU A COUPLE OF TRICKS.

CAN THEY HELP ME SPEED UP TIME? BECAUSE I CAN'T TAKE ONE MORE WEEK OF THIS TORTURE.

NEW! LIVER CHIPS

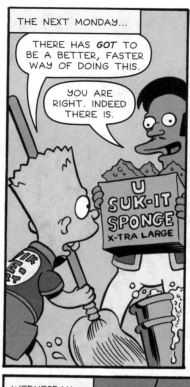

THE NEXT MONDAY...

THERE HAS *GOT* TO BE A BETTER, FASTER WAY OF DOING THIS.

YOU ARE RIGHT. INDEED THERE IS.

U SUK-IT SPONGE X-TRA LARGE

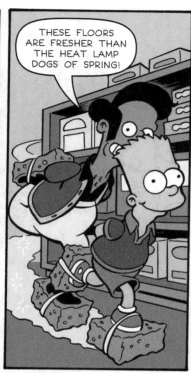

THESE FLOORS ARE FRESHER THAN THE HEAT LAMP DOGS OF SPRING!

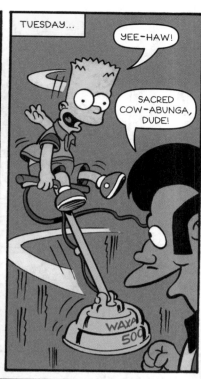

TUESDAY...

YEE-HAW!

SACRED COW-ABUNGA, DUDE!

WAXA 500

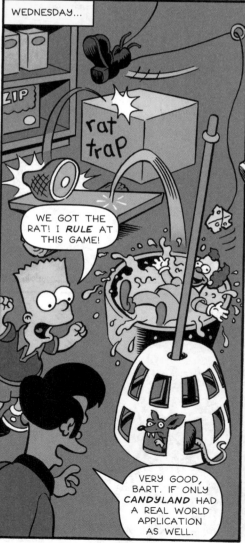

WEDNESDAY...

rat trap

ZIP

WE GOT THE RAT! I *RULE* AT THIS GAME!

VERY GOOD, BART. IF ONLY *CANDYLAND* HAD A REAL WORLD APPLICATION AS WELL.

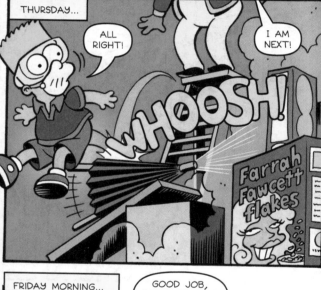

THURSDAY...

ALL RIGHT!

I AM NEXT!

WHOOSH!

Farrah Fawcett Flakes

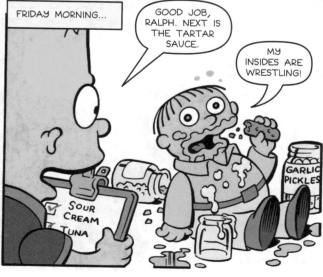

FRIDAY MORNING...

GOOD JOB, RALPH. NEXT IS THE TARTAR SAUCE.

MY INSIDES ARE WRESTLING!

SOUR CREAM TUNA

GARLIC PICKLES

LATER THAT DAY...
CHOCOLATE ONLY, CHIEF? WE DO HAVE TWO OTHER FLAVORS, YOU KNOW.
WELL, I WOULDN'T WANT THE CHOCOLATE TO GET LONELY...
DONUTS
NO CHECKS CREDIT CARDS FOOD STAMPS
I GUESS I'LL GET THE OTHERS, TOO.
SQUISH
HMM...
IT'S WHAT'S BEST FOR EVERYONE.
DONUTS
DONUTS
CHECKS CREDIT CARDS FOOD STAMPS
HEY, MR. FLANDERS, DON'T YOU NEED TO BUY SOME SMASHED PEAS TO GO WITH THAT DETERGENT?
WELL, GEE, I DON'T KNOW, BART. THAT SOUNDS TO ME LIKE A NERVOUS PURCHASE.
I HIGHLY RECOMMEND THAT YOU DO. SMASHED PEAS STAIN LIKE CRAZY AND THE DETERGENT WILL TAKE CARE OF THAT.
I NEVER QUESTION A MAN IN UNIFORM. OKILY-DOKILY! LET'S GIVE PEAS A CHANCE!
THAT'LL BE $12.95.
NO
BART, THAT WAS A MOST IMPRESSIVE DISPLAY OF SALES-MANSHIP.
YOU HAVE A REMARKABLE GIFT. YOU COULD SELL WOOL TO A SHEPHERD.
SAY WHAT?

ALMOST QUITTIN' TIME...
WATCH OUT, DIRT AND GRIME! PREPARE TO BE TERMINATED!
SUPER SQUIRTER
BART, YOU HAVE PROVEN TO BE A STELLAR EMPLOYEE THESE PAST TWO WEEKS.
I WOULD NOT WANT YOU TO QUIT NOW. IF YOU KEEP WORKING HERE, YOU COULD BE JUST LIKE ME SOMEDAY!
YO! WANNA SEE MY BULLET WOUNDS?
AAAAH!
BART, WHAT IS THE MATTER?
THANKS, APU, BUT NO THANKS. MAYBE SOMEDAY WHEN I RUN OUT OF OTHER OPTIONS.
OH, I SEE.
IT'S BEEN FUN, APU. I'LL NEVER FORGET WHAT I LEARNED.
THERE GOES A LOT OF POTENTIAL.
I GIVE IT A WEEK UNTIL HE FORGETS EVERYTHING I TAUGHT HIM.
THE END

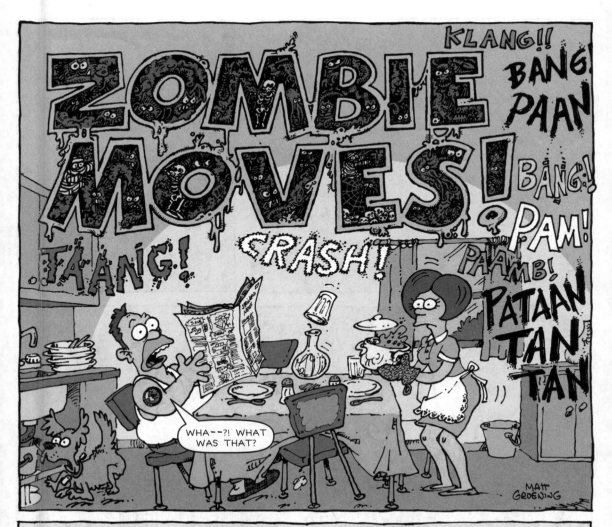

## SERGIO ARAGONES
SCRIPT & ART

## NATHAN HAMILL
COLORS

## KAREN BATES
LETTERS

## BILL MORRISON
EDITOR

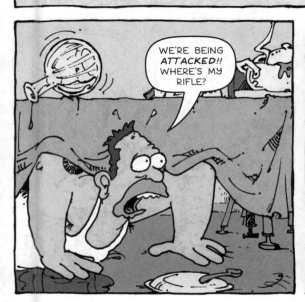

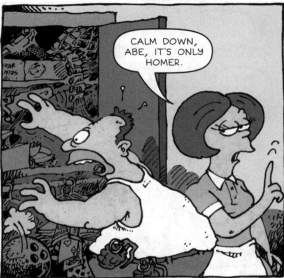

I'LL TEACH HIM TO MAKE THAT RACKET WHILE I'M AT HOME!
TWANG
BLAM!
CRASH
TAANG!
WHAT IS ALL THIS? WHAT ARE YOU DOING?
!
CLANG!
PAM! PAM!
GRAND FUNK RAILROAD
MUSIC, OF COURSE!
TAANG
TWIING!
ORANGES
BLAM!
WHY YOU LITTLE--!
BUT, DAD...
YOU'RE ALWAYS TELLING ME TO DEVELOP MY MUSICAL SKILLS!
YOU CALL THAT *MUSICAL SKILLS*?

WOULD YOU RATHER HEAR ME PLAY MY ELECTRIC GUITAR?
IS *THAT* A... ER...AN ELECTRIC GUITAR?
SURE. I MADE IT MYSELF!
HA HA! OKAY, SURE. GO AHEAD.
TELL ME, HAVE YOU PLAYED THAT THING...ER...GUITAR BEFORE?
NOPE, THIS WILL BE MY FIRST...
...TIME!!
CONCERT
HA HA HA!

HA HA! THAT WAS GREAT! NEXT TIME TRY TO MAKE AN ELECTRIC PIANO!
OR AN ELECTRIC HARMONICA! HA HA!
DING DONG!
HOMER! BARNEY'S HERE!
SO? WHAT'S UP?
GREAT NEWS!
GUESS WHAT'S COME TO SPRINGFIELD?
THE CIRCUS!
BETTER!
TWO CIRCUSES!
NO. *MUCH* BETTER!
*A MOVIE COMPANY*, AND THEY'RE FILMING ON MAIN STREET!
WHAT ARE YOU WAITING FOR!

MAYBE WE'LL SEE FAMOUS ACTORS!
OR THEY'LL ASK US TO BE ACTORS!!
THEN WE'LL MAKE THEM LISTEN TO OUR MUSIC!
AND THEN OUR BAND WILL BE FAMOUS!
MAIN
DO NOT CROSS
MAIN
RIGHT. AND I'M THE STAR OF THIS MOVIE.
DO NOT CROSS DO NOT CROSS DO NOT CRO
JUST STAY ON THAT SIDE OF THE TAPE.
MAYBE IT'S A MCBAIN MOVIE!
OR A SCHWARZENEGGER ONE!
DO NOT CROSS
A DETECTIVE MOVIE?
OR SPIES, THE END OF THE WORLD, ALIEN INVADERS DESTROYING EARTH!
DO NOT CROSS DO NOT
HMM...I WONDER WHAT KIND OF MOVIE THEY'RE SHOOTING.
I THINK I KNOW...
DO NOT CROSS

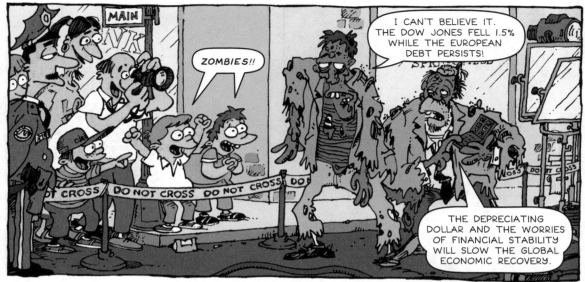

ZOMBIES!!

I CAN'T BELIEVE IT. THE DOW JONES FELL 1.5% WHILE THE EUROPEAN DEBT PERSISTS!

THE DEPRECIATING DOLLAR AND THE WORRIES OF FINANCIAL STABILITY WILL SLOW THE GLOBAL ECONOMIC RECOVERY.

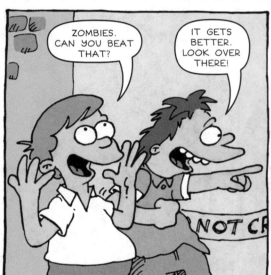

ZOMBIES. CAN YOU BEAT THAT?

IT GETS BETTER. LOOK OVER THERE!

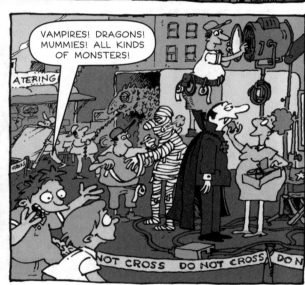

VAMPIRES! DRAGONS! MUMMIES! ALL KINDS OF MONSTERS!

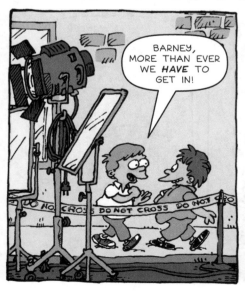

BARNEY, MORE THAN EVER WE *HAVE* TO GET IN!

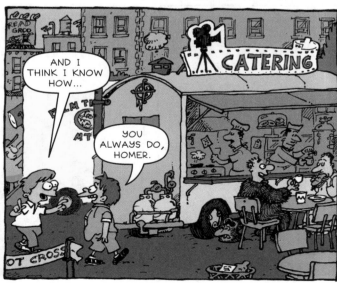

AND I THINK I KNOW HOW...

YOU ALWAYS DO, HOMER.

THE MUMMY WANTS AN ESPRESSO AND DONUTS!
AND FOR THE ZOMBIES, TWO COFFEES AND MORE DONUTS!
LET ME PASS. I'M WITH THE CATERING DELIVERY EXPRESS SERVICE.
DITTO!
DO NOT CR
WE'RE IN... AND THERE ARE PLENTY OF DONUTS!
YOUR BEST IDEA YET!
WOW! LOOK AT *THAT*!

THEY NEED MORE SMOKE AT THE OTHER END!
DEAD PEOPLE. DO NOT MOVE AFTER I SAY "ACTION!"
OVER THERE, AND DON'T BE STINGY WITH THE BLOOD!
NO. YOU ARE **NOT** A ZOMBIE. YOU'RE A DEAD GUY.
THOSE DUMMIES LOOK LIKE DUMMIES. BRING SOME DUMMIES THAT LOOK LESS LIKE DUMMIES.
AAAH!


SIR, DO WE START SENDING IN THE ZOMBIES?


BARNEY, THE ZOMBIES ARE COMING!
I ALWAYS WANTED TO BE A ZOMBIE...

WARDROBE 2
AND YOU WILL BE ONE, BARNEY!
BUT...ALL THE ZOMBIES ARE TALL!
YES, YOU'RE RIGHT. I DON'T THINK THEY USE KID ZOMBIES.
BUT I KNOW HOW TO SOLVE THAT...
EH?
ARE YOU SURE THIS IS GONNA WORK?
BUT OF COURSE, BARN. JUST HOLD STILL.
HEY, YOU!
STOP MOVING. YOU NEED MAKEUP.
YOU'RE HEAVY!
SHH!

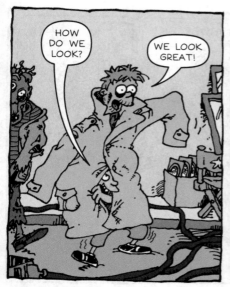

HOW DO WE LOOK?

WE LOOK GREAT!

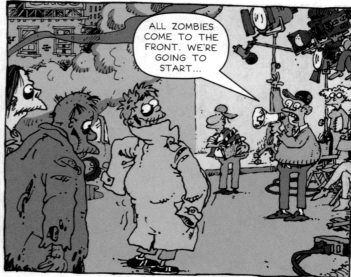

ALL ZOMBIES COME TO THE FRONT. WE'RE GOING TO START...

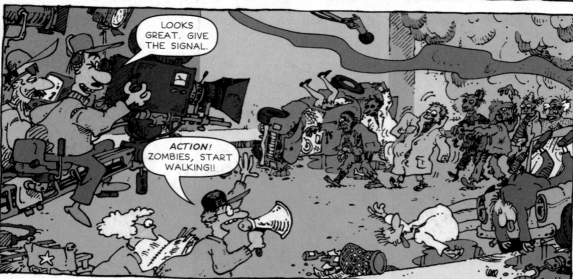

LOOKS GREAT. GIVE THE SIGNAL.

ACTION! ZOMBIES, START WALKING!!

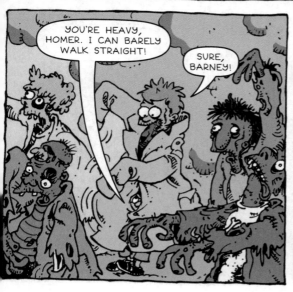

YOU'RE HEAVY, HOMER. I CAN BARELY WALK STRAIGHT!

SURE, BARNEY!

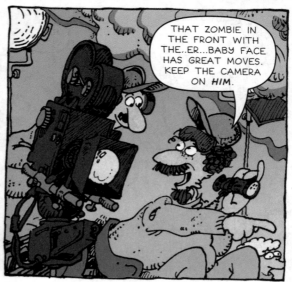

THAT ZOMBIE IN THE FRONT WITH THE..ER...BABY FACE HAS GREAT MOVES. KEEP THE CAMERA ON HIM.

STOP MOVING LIKE THAT!
I CAN'T. YOU WEIGH TOO MUCH...
OOPS, I ALMOST FELL.
AND *CUT!*
THAT WAS FUN.
WAS IT, HOMER?
BRING ME THE BABY-FACED ZOMBIE. I WANT HIM TO SHOW THE OTHER ZOMBIES HOW TO MOVE.
SURE THING, D.B.
DIRECTOR
AND HURRY. I WANT TO START SHOOTING AGAIN.
OF COURSE, D.B.

HEY, YOU!
UH-OH.
WHAT DO YOU MEAN, "UH-OH"?
RUN, BARNEY! WE'VE BEEN DISCOVERED!
GET DOWN. I'LL RUN FASTER.
WHERE DID HE GO?
I DON'T UNDERSTAND IT. THAT GUY HAD HIS CAREER MADE.
THAT WAS CLOSE. I CAN'T WAIT TO SEE THE MOVIE.
WILL I BE ABLE TO RECOGNIZE MYSELF?

A FEW MONTHS LATER...
STUDIO
PROJECTION ROOMS
THIS WAY, MICHAEL. I KNOW YOU'LL ENJOY THIS NEW HORROR MOVIE.
ROLL IT, SAM!
GREAT SCENE COMING...
HEY, THAT ZOMBIE MOVES REALLY WELL!
THOSE MOVES GIVE ME A GREAT IDEA FOR MY NEXT VIDEO...
PROJECTION
THANK YOU! GET ME THE NAME OF THAT ZOMBIE, SO I CAN SEND HIM SOME ROYALTIES!

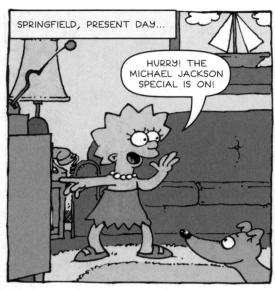

SPRINGFIELD, PRESENT DAY...

HURRY! THE MICHAEL JACKSON SPECIAL IS ON!

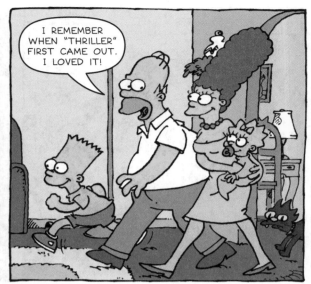

I REMEMBER WHEN "THRILLER" FIRST CAME OUT. I LOVED IT!

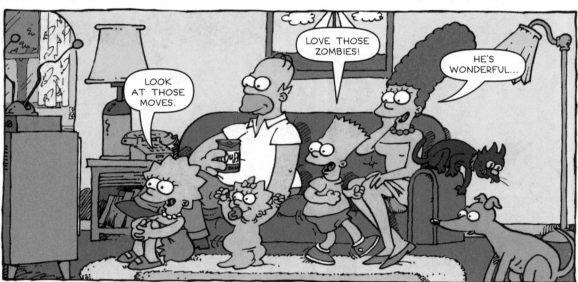

LOOK AT THOSE MOVES.

LOVE THOSE ZOMBIES!

HE'S WONDERFUL...

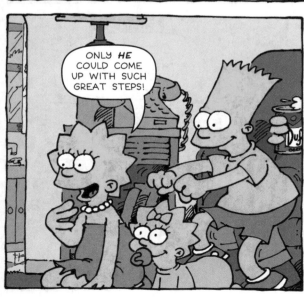

ONLY *HE* COULD COME UP WITH SUCH GREAT STEPS!

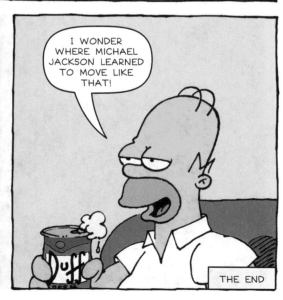

I WONDER WHERE MICHAEL JACKSON LEARNED TO MOVE LIKE THAT!

THE END

# LISA & BART SIMPSON in
# THE PRINCESS PRINCIPLE

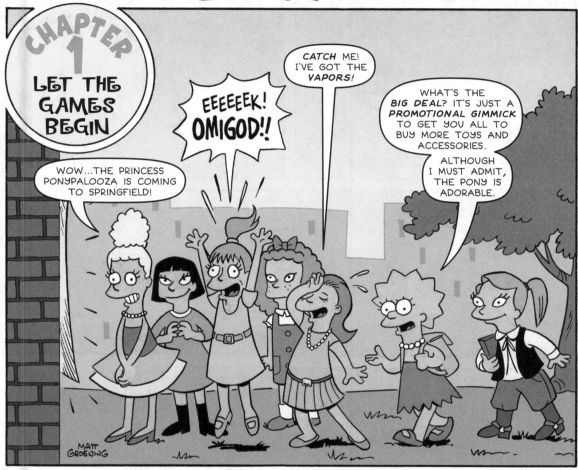

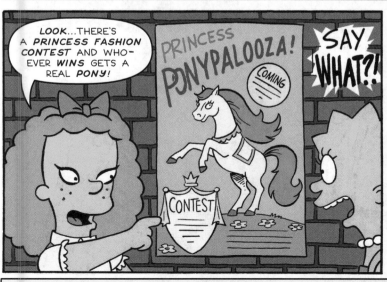

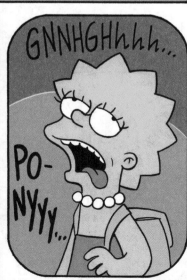

CAROL LAY
STORY & ART

ALAN HELLARD
COLORS

KAREN BATES
LETTERS

BILL MORRISON
EDITOR

WHAT... DO WE HAVE TO COMPETE AGAINST YOU, TOO? I THOUGHT YOU HATED "PRINCESS COUTURE."
COMING
CONTEST
OH! THAT'S **RIGHT** ...I **DO**!
**GOOD**. THEN WE WON'T HAVE TO COMPETE AGAINST **YOU**.
**YEAH!** YOU ALWAYS WIN EVERYTHING, GEEKAZOID.
**LOOK!** THERE'S THE **PRINCESS PONY** NOW!
I WANT TO **PET** HER!
THIS IS **PRINCESS PRECIOUS**!
SHE'S SO **BEAUTIFUL**!
NO. **I'VE** GOT TO WIN THAT PONY.
LET ME PET HER!
I'VE **GOT** TO WIN THAT PONY!
WHAT'S HER **NAME**?!

BUT HOW CAN I JOIN SUCH A REPREHENSIBLE CONTEST?
NOT ONLY DOES THE PRINCESS PHENOMENON PROMOTE UNATTAINABLE FANTASIES AND THE SHALLOW ACQUISITION OF MATERIAL GOODS...
...BUT THE CONTEST PITS GIRLS AGAINST EACH OTHER WHEN WE SHOULD BE SUPPORTING EACH OTHER'S GOALS AND ASPIRATIONS.
I'M NEXT!
GET BENT!
PP
LISA, YOU AND I ARE MEANT TO BE TOGETHER.
YES. I FEEL THAT, TOO!
LET US RUN FREE AND WILD, ESCHEWING THIS PROVINCIAL BACKWATER!
WOW! YOU'RE NOT JUST A PRETTY FACE...YOU HAVE A TERRIFIC VOCABULARY!

OUR MINDS AND HEARTS ARE AS ONE!
I EVEN LIKE "ITCHY AND SCRATCHY!"
YOU'RE PERFECT! I LOVE YOU!
BUT HOW CAN I WIN YOU? I'D HAVE TO BETRAY MY PRINCIPLES!
YOU WILL FIND A WAY.
GALLOP GALLOP GALLOP
YES, I'M CLEVER ENOUGH TO JUSTIFY ALMOST ANYTHING!
THAT'S MY GIRL! GO FORTH AND KICK SOME HIND-QUARTERS!
YES! I WILL CRUSH YOU ALL AND WIN THIS PONY!
PP
DID I SAY THAT ALOUD?
SAY WHAT, EGGHEAD?
HEE HEE HEH. NOTHING...
GOOD. I'M GLAD THEY DIDN'T HEAR ME BECAUSE--
SHUT UP, NERD.
OOPS.

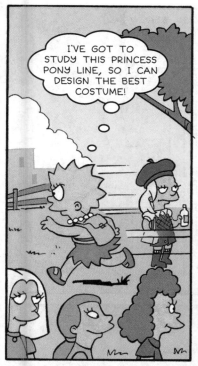

I'VE GOT TO STUDY THIS PRINCESS PONY LINE, SO I CAN DESIGN THE BEST COSTUME!

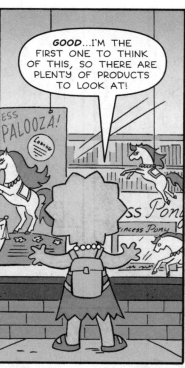

GOOD...I'M THE FIRST ONE TO THINK OF THIS, SO THERE ARE PLENTY OF PRODUCTS TO LOOK AT!

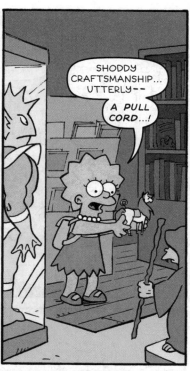

SHODDY CRAFTSMANSHIP... UTTERLY--

A PULL CORD...!

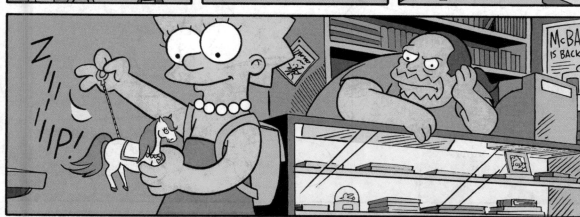

Z...IP!

McBA IS BACK

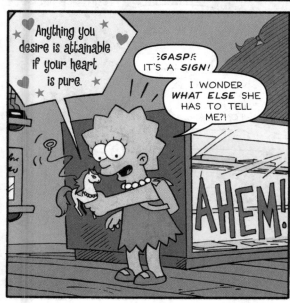

Anything you desire is attainable if your heart is pure.

≧GASP≦ IT'S A SIGN!

I WONDER WHAT ELSE SHE HAS TO TELL ME?!

AHEM!

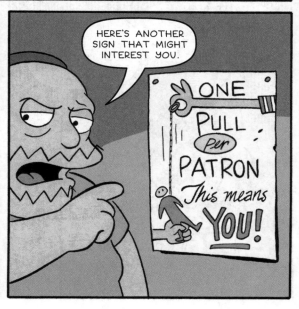

HERE'S ANOTHER SIGN THAT MIGHT INTEREST YOU.

ONE PULL per PATRON This means YOU!

I'VE **GOT** TO KNOW WHAT **ELSE** SHE'LL SAY!
I HOPE I HAVE ENOUGH BABYSITTING MONEY...
Stacy
BUMP!
**MALIBU STACY!**
I'M NOT BETRAYING YOU... **REALLY!**
Stacy
WHATEVER YOU DREAM CAN BECOME REALITY IF YOU APPLY YOUR INTELLECT.
MAYBE THEY'RE **BOTH** RIGHT!
I'VE BEEN WAITING FOR YOU TO CROSS OVER TO THE PINK AND GIRLY SIDE, YOUNG LADY.
HAVE YOU SEEN THE LATEST PRINCESS PONY BOUDOIR BEAUTY SET? ONLY $37.99 PLUS TAX.
IT'S SO VAPIDLY POINTLESS!
BUT IT'S **PRETTY!** I WANT IT!
KA-CHING! THAT IS MUSIC TO MY POINTY VULCAN EARS.
Princess Pony
Boudoir Beauty

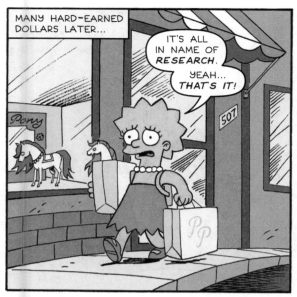

MANY HARD-EARNED DOLLARS LATER...

IT'S ALL IN NAME OF *RESEARCH*. YEAH... *THAT'S IT!*

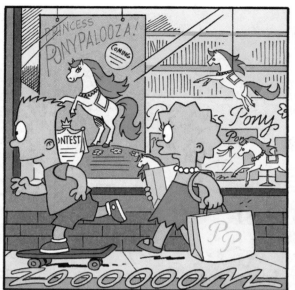

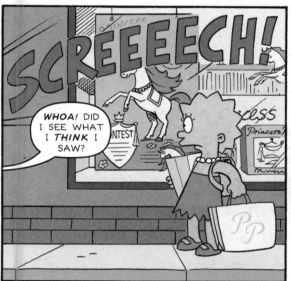

*SCREEEECH!*

*WHOA!* DID I SEE WHAT I *THINK* I SAW?

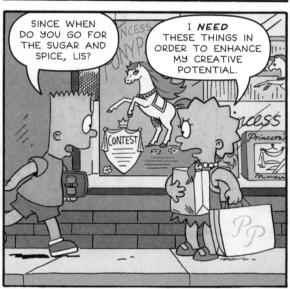

SINCE WHEN DO YOU GO FOR THE SUGAR AND SPICE, LIS?

I *NEED* THESE THINGS IN ORDER TO ENHANCE MY CREATIVE POTENTIAL.

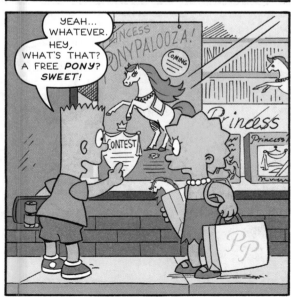

YEAH... WHATEVER. HEY, WHAT'S THAT? A FREE *PONY? SWEET!*

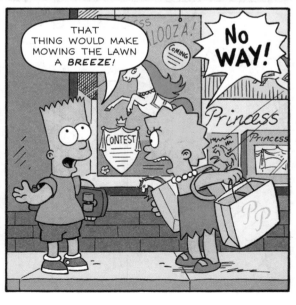

THAT THING WOULD MAKE MOWING THE LAWN A *BREEZE!*

*NO WAY!*

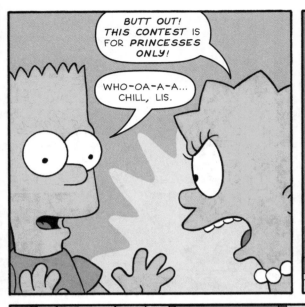

BUTT OUT! *THIS CONTEST* IS FOR *PRINCESSES ONLY!*

WHO-OA-A-A... CHILL, LIS.

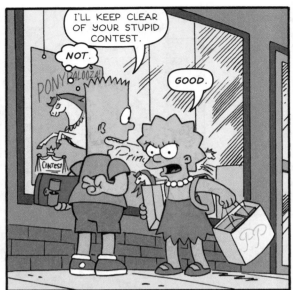

I'LL KEEP CLEAR OF YOUR STUPID CONTEST.

*NOT.*

GOOD.

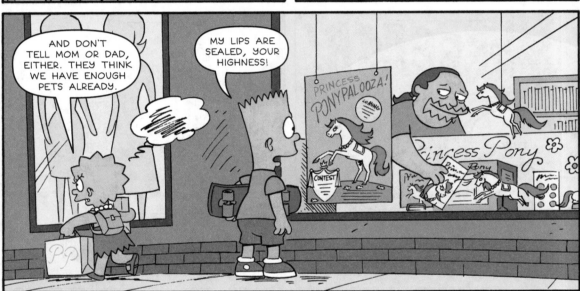

AND DON'T TELL MOM OR DAD, EITHER. THEY THINK WE HAVE ENOUGH PETS ALREADY.

MY LIPS ARE SEALED, YOUR HIGHNESS!

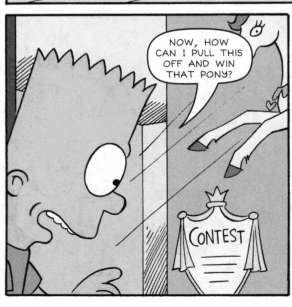

NOW, HOW CAN I PULL THIS OFF AND WIN THAT PONY?

CONTEST

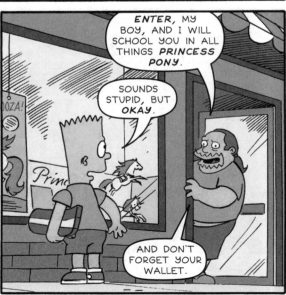

*ENTER,* MY BOY, AND I WILL SCHOOL YOU IN ALL THINGS *PRINCESS PONY.*

SOUNDS STUPID, BUT *OKAY.*

AND DON'T FORGET YOUR WALLET.

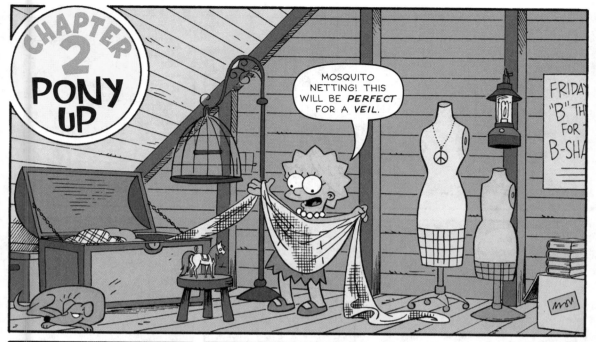

MOSQUITO NETTING! THIS WILL BE *PERFECT* FOR A *VEIL*.

FRIDAY "B" TH FOR T B-SHA

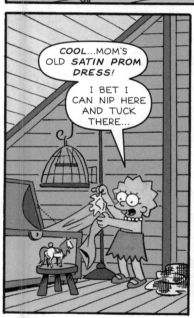

COOL...MOM'S OLD *SATIN PROM DRESS!*

I BET I CAN NIP HERE AND TUCK THERE...

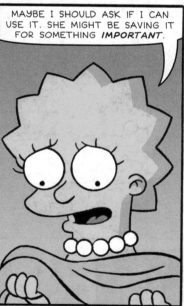

MAYBE I SHOULD ASK IF I CAN USE IT. SHE MIGHT BE SAVING IT FOR SOMETHING *IMPORTANT*.

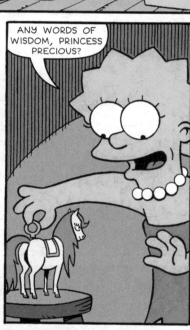

ANY WORDS OF WISDOM, PRINCESS PRECIOUS?

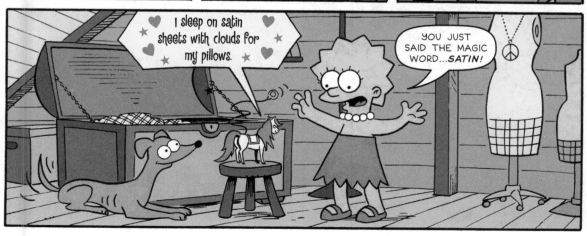

♥ I sleep on satin ♥ sheets with clouds for ★ my pillows. ★ ♥

YOU JUST SAID THE MAGIC WORD...*SATIN!*

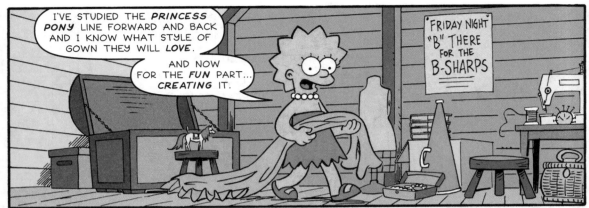

I'VE STUDIED THE **PRINCESS PONY** LINE FORWARD AND BACK AND I KNOW WHAT STYLE OF GOWN THEY WILL **LOVE**.

AND NOW FOR THE **FUN** PART... **CREATING** IT.

"FRIDAY NIGHT "B" THERE FOR THE B-SHARPS

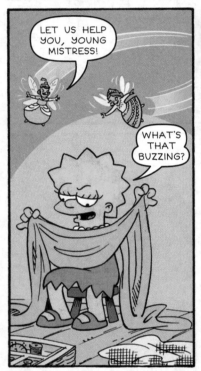

LET US HELP YOU, YOUNG MISTRESS!

WHAT'S THAT BUZZING?

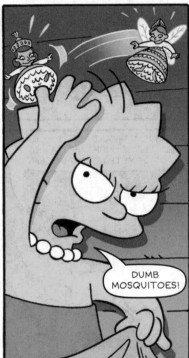

DUMB MOSQUITOES!

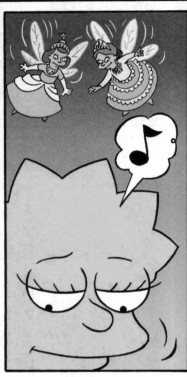

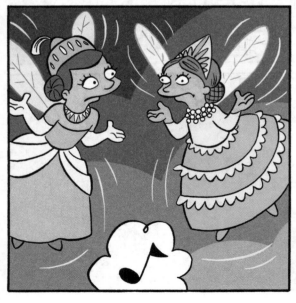

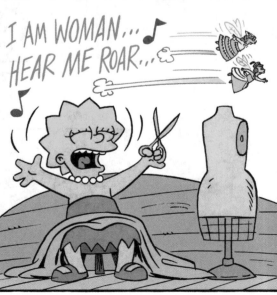

I AM WOMAN... HEAR ME ROAR...

NOW I'M A MAN... I SPELL M-A-N... MAN.
THE STAINS ON THESE OVERALLS LOOK KINDA LIKE LEOPARD SPOTS. HOW ROYAL CAN YOU GET?
SPAGHETTI
LET US HELP YOU, YOUNG MASTER!
WHAT'S THAT SQUEAKING?
HEY! BEAT IT!
SPAGHETTI
THEY PROBABLY SMELLED THIS SPAGHETTI I'M GOING TO USE FOR HAIR.
HEH HEH. STUPID CHEESE EATERS.
SNAP! SNAP!
NOW I'M A MAN...I SPELL M-

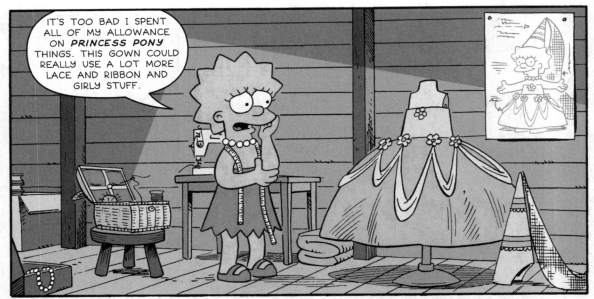

IT'S TOO BAD I SPENT ALL OF MY ALLOWANCE ON *PRINCESS PONY* THINGS. THIS GOWN COULD REALLY USE A LOT MORE LACE AND RIBBON AND GIRLY STUFF.

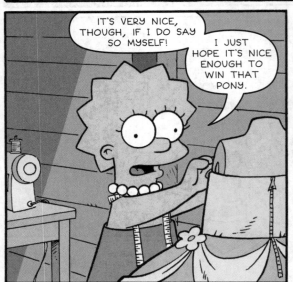

IT'S VERY NICE, THOUGH, IF I DO SAY SO MYSELF!

I JUST HOPE IT'S NICE ENOUGH TO WIN THAT PONY.

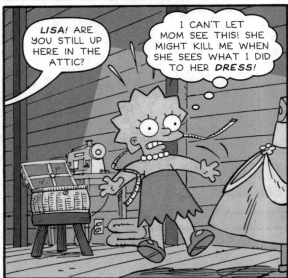

*LISA!* ARE YOU STILL UP HERE IN THE ATTIC?

I CAN'T LET MOM SEE THIS! SHE MIGHT KILL ME WHEN SHE SEES WHAT I DID TO HER *DRESS!*

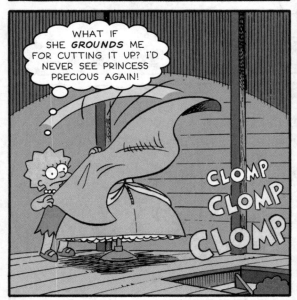

WHAT IF SHE *GROUNDS* ME FOR CUTTING IT UP? I'D NEVER SEE PRINCESS PRECIOUS AGAIN!

CLOMP
CLOMP
CLOMP

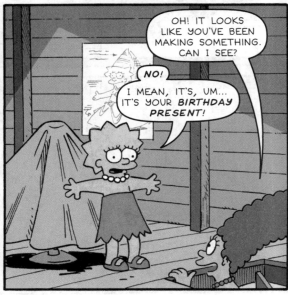

OH! IT LOOKS LIKE YOU'VE BEEN MAKING SOMETHING. CAN I SEE?

*NO!*

I MEAN, IT'S, UM... IT'S YOUR *BIRTHDAY PRESENT!*

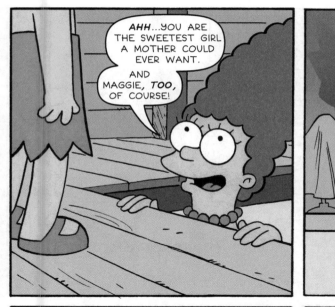

AHH...YOU ARE THE SWEETEST GIRL A MOTHER COULD EVER WANT.

AND MAGGIE, *TOO,* OF COURSE!

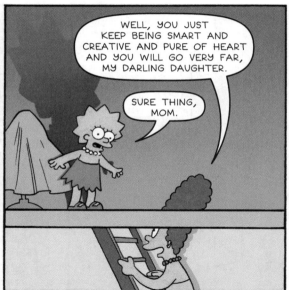

WELL, YOU JUST KEEP BEING SMART AND CREATIVE AND PURE OF HEART AND YOU WILL GO VERY FAR, MY DARLING DAUGHTER.

SURE THING, MOM.

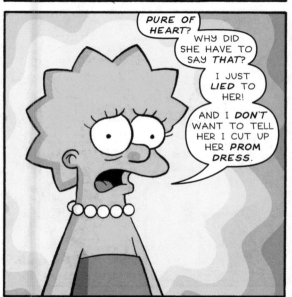

*PURE OF HEART?* WHY DID SHE HAVE TO SAY *THAT?*

I JUST *LIED* TO HER!

AND I *DON'T* WANT TO TELL HER I CUT UP HER *PROM DRESS.*

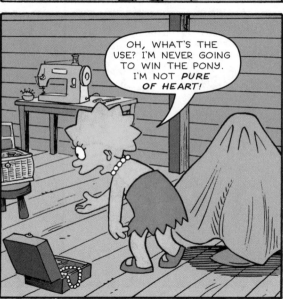

OH, WHAT'S THE USE? I'M NEVER GOING TO WIN THE PONY. I'M NOT *PURE OF HEART!*

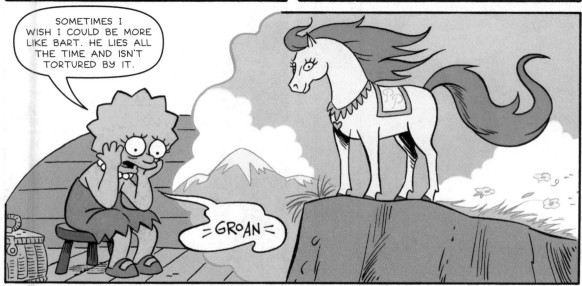

SOMETIMES I WISH I COULD BE MORE LIKE BART. HE LIES ALL THE TIME AND ISN'T TORTURED BY IT.

=GROAN=

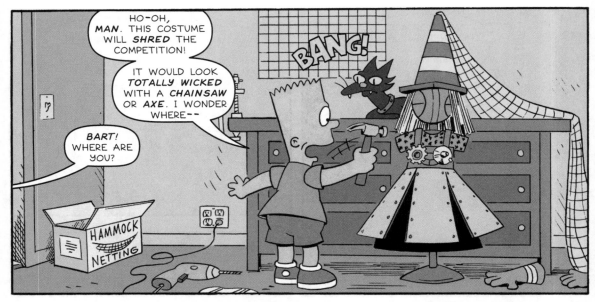

HO-OH, *MAN*. THIS COSTUME WILL *SHRED* THE COMPETITION!

IT WOULD LOOK *TOTALLY WICKED* WITH A *CHAINSAW* OR *AXE*. I WONDER WHERE--

*BART!* WHERE ARE YOU?

BANG!

HAMMOCK NETTING

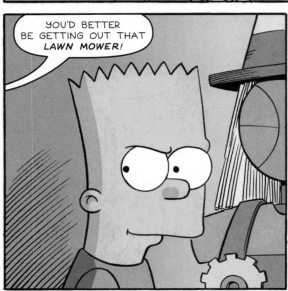

YOU'D BETTER BE GETTING OUT THAT *LAWN MOWER!*

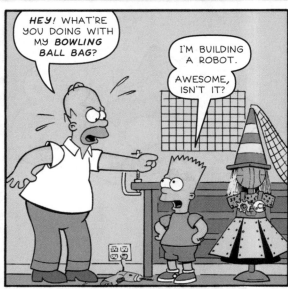

*HEY!* WHAT'RE YOU DOING WITH MY *BOWLING BALL BAG?*

I'M BUILDING A ROBOT. AWESOME, ISN'T IT?

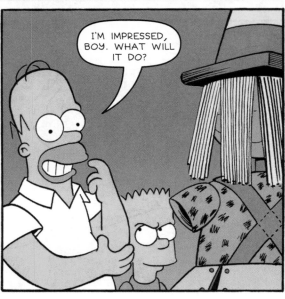

I'M IMPRESSED, BOY. WHAT WILL IT DO?

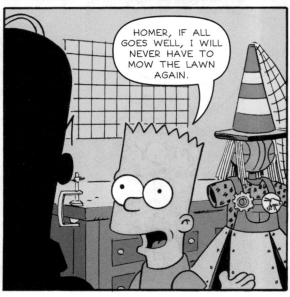

HOMER, IF ALL GOES WELL, I WILL NEVER HAVE TO MOW THE LAWN AGAIN.

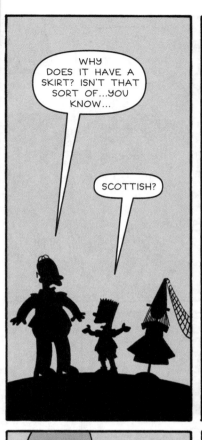

WHY DOES IT HAVE A SKIRT? ISN'T THAT SORT OF...YOU KNOW...

SCOTTISH?

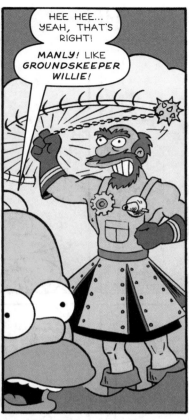

HEE HEE... YEAH, THAT'S RIGHT!

*MANLY!* LIKE *GROUNDSKEEPER WILLIE!*

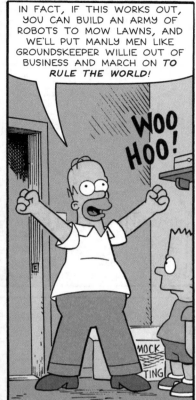

IN FACT, IF THIS WORKS OUT, YOU CAN BUILD AN ARMY OF ROBOTS TO MOW LAWNS, AND WE'LL PUT MANLY MEN LIKE GROUNDSKEEPER WILLIE OUT OF BUSINESS AND MARCH ON *TO RULE THE WORLD!*

WOO HOO!

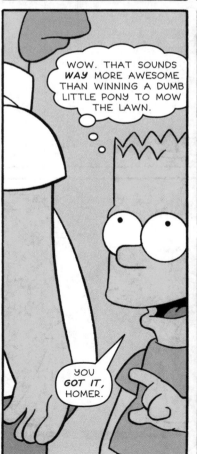

WOW. THAT SOUNDS *WAY* MORE AWESOME THAN WINNING A DUMB LITTLE PONY TO MOW THE LAWN.

YOU *GOT IT,* HOMER.

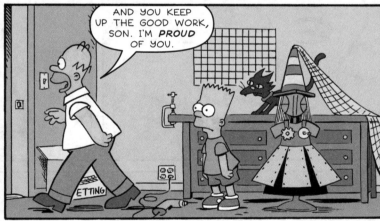

AND YOU KEEP UP THE GOOD WORK, SON. I'M *PROUD* OF YOU.

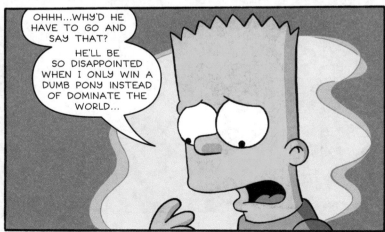

OHHH...WHY'D HE HAVE TO GO AND SAY THAT?

HE'LL BE SO DISAPPOINTED WHEN I ONLY WIN A DUMB PONY INSTEAD OF DOMINATE THE WORLD...

AW, SO WHAT? HOMER'S DISAPPOINTED IN ME ALL THE TIME.
I WOULDN'T WANT TO UPSET THE NATURAL ORDER OF THINGS.
HAMMOCK NETTING
IT'S TIME TO TAKE THIS BABY OUT FOR A TEST DRIVE.
THIS HOCKEY MASK WILL HELP DISGUISE ME. NO ONE CAN FIND OUT I'M NOT A GIRL.
AS IF.
WHOA!
OH, MAN. I AM SUDDENLY NOT SO SURE OF MY CHANCES OF WINNING EVEN THAT DUMB LITTLE PONY.

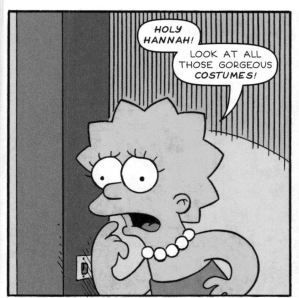

HOLY *HANNAH!*

LOOK AT ALL THOSE GORGEOUS *COSTUMES!*

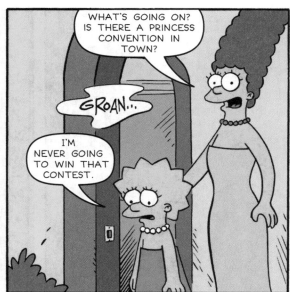

WHAT'S GOING ON? IS THERE A PRINCESS CONVENTION IN TOWN?

GROAN...

I'M NEVER GOING TO WIN THAT CONTEST.

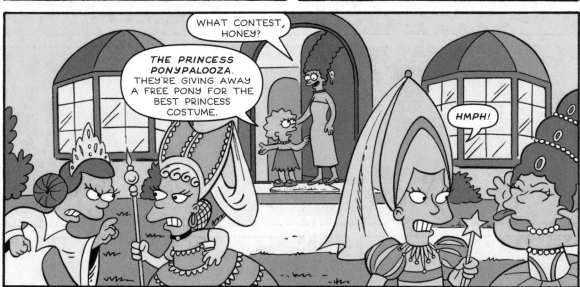

WHAT CONTEST, HONEY?

*THE PRINCESS PONYPALOOZA.* THEY'RE GIVING AWAY A FREE PONY FOR THE BEST PRINCESS COSTUME.

HMPH!

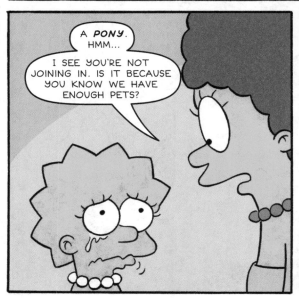

A *PONY.* HMM...

I SEE YOU'RE NOT JOINING IN. IS IT BECAUSE YOU KNOW WE HAVE ENOUGH PETS?

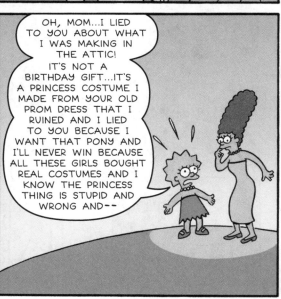

OH, MOM...I LIED TO YOU ABOUT WHAT I WAS MAKING IN THE ATTIC! IT'S NOT A BIRTHDAY GIFT...IT'S A PRINCESS COSTUME I MADE FROM YOUR OLD PROM DRESS THAT I RUINED AND I LIED TO YOU BECAUSE I WANT THAT PONY AND I'LL NEVER WIN BECAUSE ALL THESE GIRLS BOUGHT REAL COSTUMES AND I KNOW THE PRINCESS THING IS STUPID AND WRONG AND--

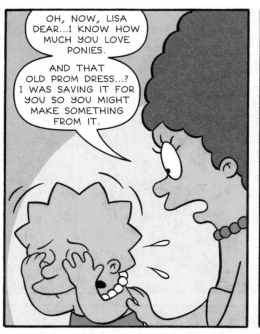

OH, NOW, LISA DEAR...I KNOW HOW MUCH YOU LOVE PONIES.

AND THAT OLD PROM DRESS...? I WAS SAVING IT FOR YOU SO YOU MIGHT MAKE SOMETHING FROM IT.

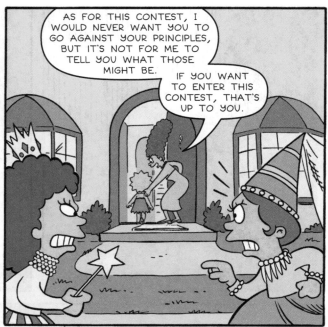

AS FOR THIS CONTEST, I WOULD NEVER WANT YOU TO GO AGAINST YOUR PRINCIPLES, BUT IT'S NOT FOR ME TO TELL YOU WHAT THOSE MIGHT BE.

IF YOU WANT TO ENTER THIS CONTEST, THAT'S UP TO YOU.

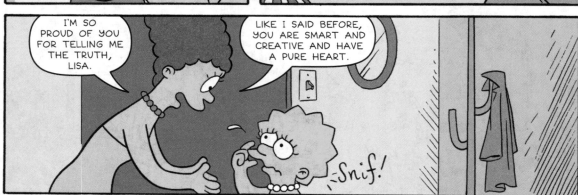

I'M SO PROUD OF YOU FOR TELLING ME THE TRUTH, LISA.

LIKE I SAID BEFORE, YOU ARE SMART AND CREATIVE AND HAVE A PURE HEART.

*Snif!*

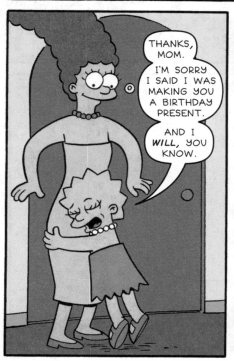

THANKS, MOM.

I'M SORRY I SAID I WAS MAKING YOU A BIRTHDAY PRESENT.

AND I *WILL*, YOU KNOW.

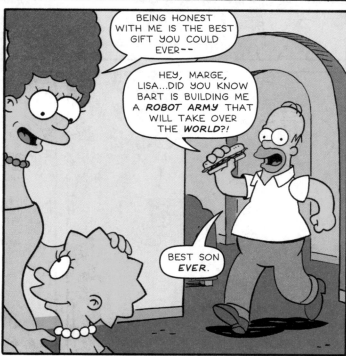

BEING HONEST WITH ME IS THE BEST GIFT YOU COULD EVER--

HEY, MARGE, LISA...DID YOU KNOW BART IS BUILDING ME A *ROBOT ARMY* THAT WILL TAKE OVER THE *WORLD*?!

BEST SON *EVER*.

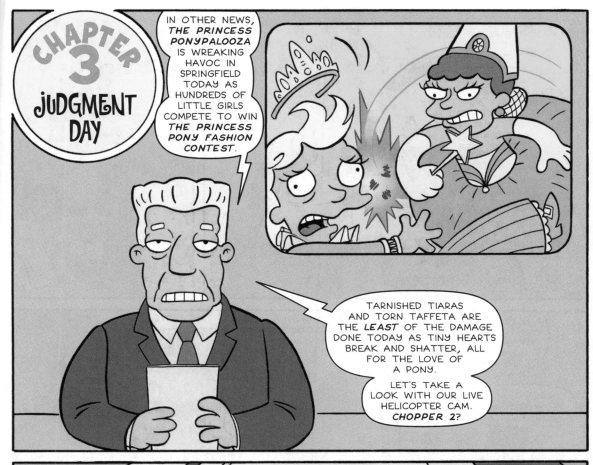

CHAPTER **3**
JUDGMENT DAY

IN OTHER NEWS, *THE PRINCESS PONYPALOOZA* IS WREAKING HAVOC IN SPRINGFIELD TODAY AS HUNDREDS OF LITTLE GIRLS COMPETE TO WIN *THE PRINCESS PONY FASHION CONTEST.*

TARNISHED TIARAS AND TORN TAFFETA ARE THE *LEAST* OF THE DAMAGE DONE TODAY AS TINY HEARTS BREAK AND SHATTER, ALL FOR THE LOVE OF A PONY.

LET'S TAKE A LOOK WITH OUR LIVE HELICOPTER CAM. *CHOPPER 2?*

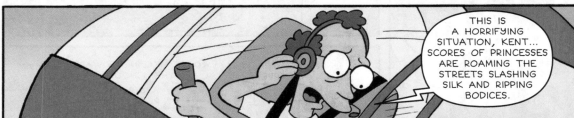

THIS IS A HORRIFYING SITUATION, KENT... SCORES OF PRINCESSES ARE ROAMING THE STREETS SLASHING SILK AND RIPPING BODICES.

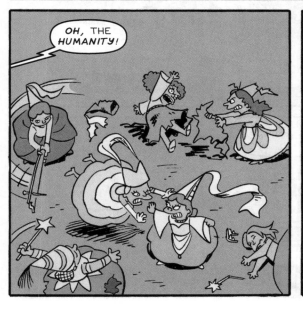

OH, THE *HUMANITY!*

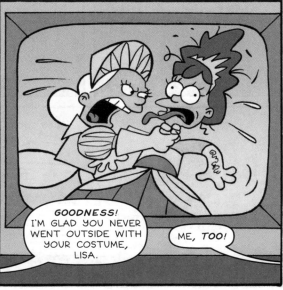

*GOODNESS!* I'M GLAD YOU NEVER WENT OUTSIDE WITH YOUR COSTUME, LISA.

ME, *TOO!*

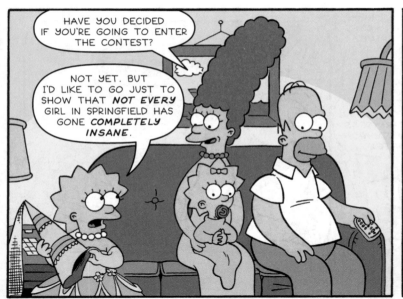

HAVE YOU DECIDED IF YOU'RE GOING TO ENTER THE CONTEST?

NOT YET. BUT I'D LIKE TO GO JUST TO SHOW THAT *NOT EVERY* GIRL IN SPRINGFIELD HAS GONE *COMPLETELY INSANE.*

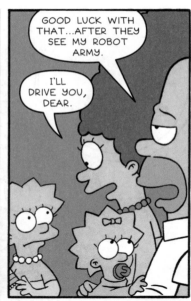

GOOD LUCK WITH THAT...AFTER THEY SEE MY ROBOT ARMY.

I'LL DRIVE YOU, DEAR.

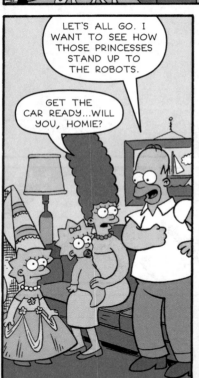

LET'S ALL GO. I WANT TO SEE HOW THOSE PRINCESSES STAND UP TO THE ROBOTS.

GET THE CAR READY...WILL YOU, HOMIE?

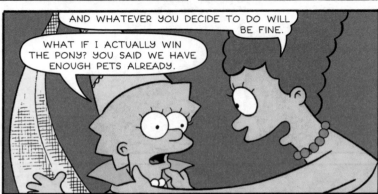

AND WHATEVER YOU DECIDE TO DO WILL BE FINE.

WHAT IF I ACTUALLY WIN THE PONY? YOU SAID WE HAVE ENOUGH PETS ALREADY.

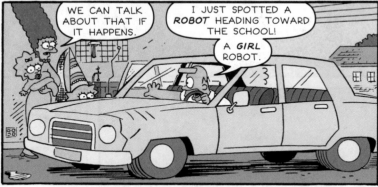

WE CAN TALK ABOUT THAT IF IT HAPPENS.

I JUST SPOTTED A *ROBOT* HEADING TOWARD THE SCHOOL!

A *GIRL* ROBOT.

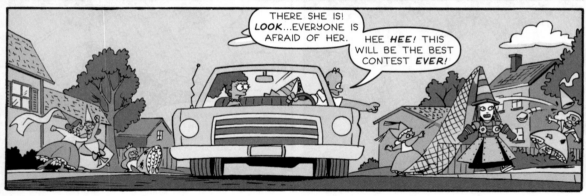

THERE SHE IS! *LOOK*...EVERYONE IS AFRAID OF HER.

HEE *HEE!* THIS WILL BE THE BEST CONTEST *EVER!*

WHAT DO YOU MEAN, WE HAVE TO SHUT DOWN THE CONTEST?
THE PRINCESS PONY COMPANY GAVE YOUR SCHOOL DISTRICT GOOD MONEY SO WE COULD PROMOTE THIS EVENT!
DEAR GOD, I'M HAVING A FLASHBACK.
LISTEN HERE, COUNTLESS LITTLE GIRLS ARE TRAUMATIZED FOR LIFE, RIPPING OFF THEIR OWN GOWNS TO KEEP FROM BEING ATTACKED BY POINTY-TOPPED LITTLE SAVAGES WITH WANDS.
MEDIC!
YOU SIGNED A CONTRACT, CHALMERS, AND WE'RE HOLDING YOU TO IT!
PRINCESS PRECIOUS...
WE DID THIS...FOR YOU...
AND AS LONG AS WE HAVE AT LEAST TWO VIABLE CONTESTANTS, WE HAVE A CONTEST!
LOOK! THERE'S ONE NOW!
AND YOUR SECOND CONTESTANT IS RIGHT HERE.

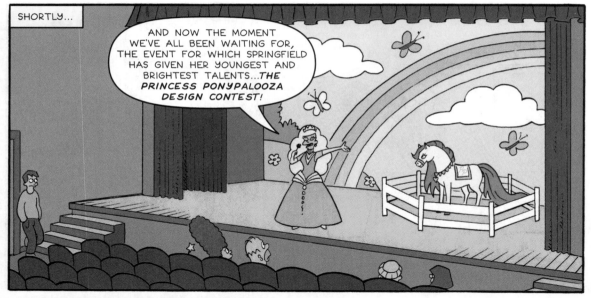

AND NOW THE MOMENT WE'VE ALL BEEN WAITING FOR, THE EVENT FOR WHICH SPRINGFIELD HAS GIVEN HER YOUNGEST AND BRIGHTEST TALENTS...*THE PRINCESS PONYPALOOZA DESIGN CONTEST!*

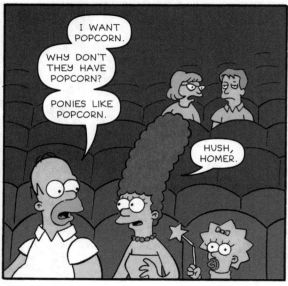

I WANT POPCORN.

WHY DON'T THEY HAVE POPCORN?

PONIES LIKE POPCORN.

HUSH, HOMER.

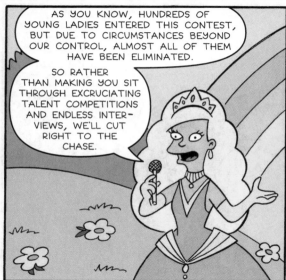

AS YOU KNOW, HUNDREDS OF YOUNG LADIES ENTERED THIS CONTEST, BUT DUE TO CIRCUMSTANCES BEYOND OUR CONTROL, ALMOST ALL OF THEM HAVE BEEN ELIMINATED.

SO RATHER THAN MAKING YOU SIT THROUGH EXCRUCIATING TALENT COMPETITIONS AND ENDLESS INTER-VIEWS, WE'LL CUT RIGHT TO THE CHASE.

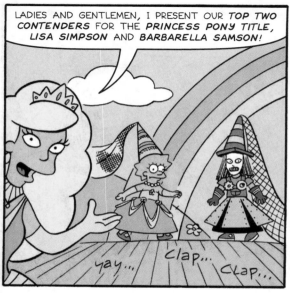

LADIES AND GENTLEMEN, I PRESENT OUR *TOP TWO CONTENDERS* FOR THE *PRINCESS PONY TITLE*, *LISA SIMPSON* AND *BARBARELLA SAMSON!*

*Yay...*

*Clap...*

*Clap...*

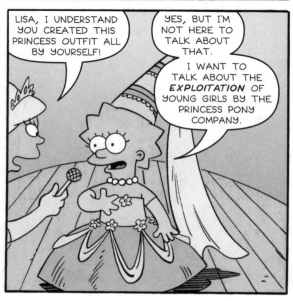

LISA, I UNDERSTAND YOU CREATED THIS PRINCESS OUTFIT ALL BY YOURSELF!

YES, BUT I'M NOT HERE TO TALK ABOUT THAT.

I WANT TO TALK ABOUT THE *EXPLOITATION* OF YOUNG GIRLS BY THE PRINCESS PONY COMPANY.

WHAT?! SHE CAN'T SAY THAT!
I'LL GO TALK TO THE JUDGES!
BARBARELLA WINS. GOT IT?
$ $
AND FOR ANOTHER SURPRISE IN AN EVER-SURPRISING CONTEST, WE HAVE A WINNER!
BARBARELLA
Barbarella
Babs
LADIES AND GENTLEMEN, THE NEWEST PRINCESS PONYPALOOZA PRINCESS IS...BARBARELLA SAMSON!
HUH? NO WAY!
I GET THE PONY?!
SNIF
I'D LIKE TO THANK--
NIP!
HEY! WATCH THE CHOPPERS, YOU DUMB ANIMAL!

BART! YOU CAN'T BE IN THIS CONTEST! YOU'RE NOT A GIRL!
AND PRECIOUS IS NOT A DUMB ANIMAL!
CHOMP!
WELL, IT SEEMS LISA SIMPSON WINS, AFTER ALL. CONGRATULATIONS.
I KNOW YOU'D LIKE TO SAY A FEW WORDS, BUT WE'RE OUT OF TIME.
GIVE ME THAT!
I HOPE YOU CAN HEAR ME PAST THE FIRST ROW...? WHAT I HAVE TO SAY IS IMPORTANT!
I WENT AGAINST ALL I HOLD DEAR TO WIN THIS CONTEST.
I LIED TO MY MOM, AND I BETRAYED MY PRINCIPLES.
I COMPETED WITH OTHER GIRLS INSTEAD OF SUPPORTING MY SISTERS.
AND IN SPITE OF ALL THAT, I'M GLAD I DECIDED TO ENTER THIS CONTEST, IF ONLY TO SAVE THE PONY FROM THE DRUDGERY OF MOWING LAWNS.
I KNOW YOU HAVE TV PROGRAMS YOU'RE EAGER TO GO HOME TO, SO I'LL CONCLUDE WITH THIS...
...IN YOUR FACE, BART!

LATER...
YOU DID A WONDERFUL THING, LISA, GIVING PRECIOUS TO THE PONY PROTECTION PEOPLE.
SHE'LL PLAY IN GREEN PASTURES AND NEVER HAVE TO WEAR A SADDLE OR HARNESS AS LONG AS SHE LIVES.
IF PONIES WEREN'T MEANT TO CARRY PEOPLE, HOW COME SADDLES FIT THEM SO GOOD?
YEAH!
HE-E-E-Y-Y-Y... YOU SAID YOU WERE BUILDING ME A ROBOT ARMY WHEN YOU WERE REALLY USING MY STUFF TO MAKE A GIRLY COSTUME.
C'MON, HOMER. YOU THINK THIS LOOKS GIRLY?
IT'S GOT A SKIRT.
OKAY, WAIT...
FWIP!
FOOSH!
THAT'S MORE LIKE IT, SON!
I LOVE YOU, TOO, MAN.
THE END

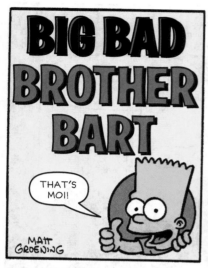

# BIG BAD BROTHER BART

THAT'S MOI!

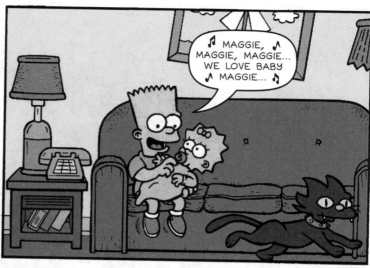

♪ MAGGIE, MAGGIE, MAGGIE... WE LOVE BABY MAGGIE... ♪

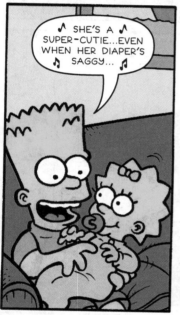

♪ SHE'S A ♪ SUPER-CUTIE...EVEN WHEN HER DIAPER'S SAGGY... ♪

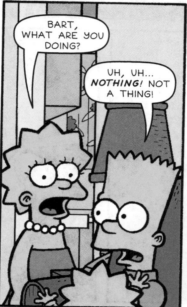

BART, WHAT ARE YOU DOING?

UH, UH... *NOTHING!* NOT A THING!

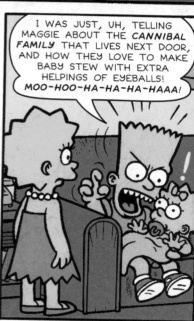

I WAS JUST, UH, TELLING MAGGIE ABOUT THE *CANNIBAL FAMILY* THAT LIVES NEXT DOOR, AND HOW THEY LOVE TO MAKE BABY STEW WITH EXTRA HELPINGS OF EYEBALLS! *MOO-HOO-HA-HA-HA-HAAA!*

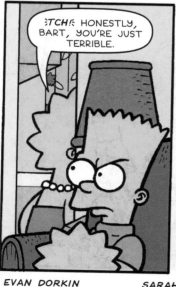

*TCH!* HONESTLY, BART, YOU'RE JUST TERRIBLE.

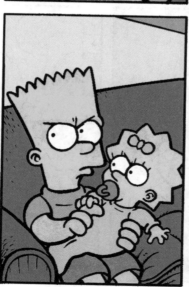

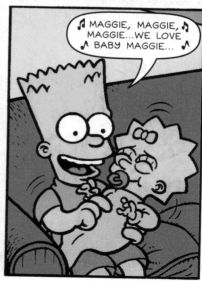

♪ MAGGIE, MAGGIE, MAGGIE...WE LOVE ♪ BABY MAGGIE... ♪

**EVAN DORKIN**
SCRIPT & ART

**SARAH DYER**
COLORS

**KAREN BATES**
LETTERS

**BILL MORRISON**
EDITOR

# BART & LISA SIMPSON with RALPH WIGGUM in

# MAIL-ORDER MAYHEM!

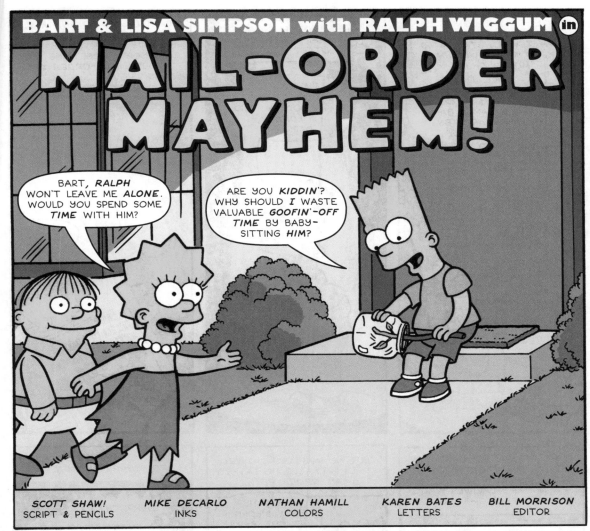

**BART, RALPH** WON'T LEAVE ME **ALONE.** WOULD YOU SPEND SOME **TIME** WITH HIM?

ARE YOU **KIDDIN'**? WHY SHOULD **I** WASTE VALUABLE **GOOFIN'-OFF TIME** BY BABYSITTING **HIM**?

| **SCOTT SHAW!** SCRIPT & PENCILS | **MIKE DECARLO** INKS | **NATHAN HAMILL** COLORS | **KAREN BATES** LETTERS | **BILL MORRISON** EDITOR |

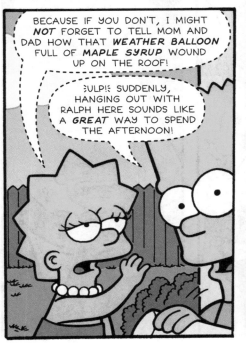

BECAUSE IF YOU DON'T, I MIGHT **NOT** FORGET TO TELL MOM AND DAD HOW THAT **WEATHER BALLOON** FULL OF **MAPLE SYRUP** WOUND UP ON THE ROOF!

:GULP!: SUDDENLY, HANGING OUT WITH RALPH HERE SOUNDS LIKE A **GREAT** WAY TO SPEND THE AFTERNOON!

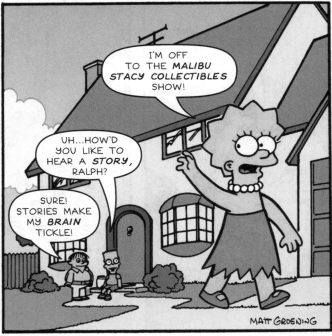

I'M OFF TO THE **MALIBU STACY COLLECTIBLES** SHOW!

UH...HOW'D YOU LIKE TO HEAR A **STORY,** RALPH?

SURE! STORIES MAKE MY **BRAIN** TICKLE!

MATT GROENING

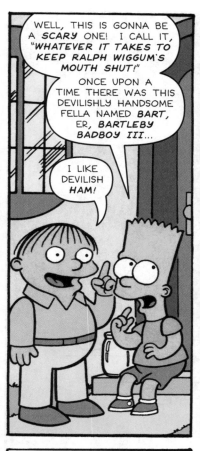

WELL, THIS IS GONNA BE A *SCARY* ONE! I CALL IT, *"WHATEVER IT TAKES TO KEEP RALPH WIGGUM'S MOUTH SHUT!"*

ONCE UPON A TIME THERE WAS THIS DEVILISHLY HANDSOME FELLA NAMED *BART*, ER, *BARTLEBY BADBOY III...*

I LIKE DEVILISH *HAM!*

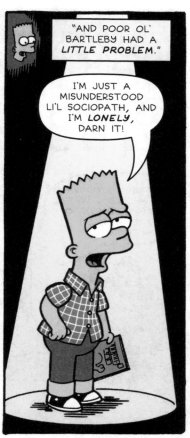

*"AND POOR OL' BARTLEBY HAD A LITTLE PROBLEM."*

I'M JUST A MISUNDERSTOOD LI'L SOCIOPATH, AND I'M *LONELY*, DARN IT!

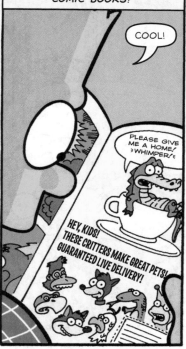

*"BARTLEBY LOVED ANIMALS, BUT HIS PARENTS WOULDN'T BUY HIM A PET...SO HE HAD TO RESORT TO GETTING ONE THROUGH MAIL-ORDER ADS IN THE BACK OF OLD COMIC BOOKS!"*

COOL!

PLEASE GIVE ME A HOME! ≈WHIMPER!≈

HEY, KIDS! THESE CRITTERS MAKE GREAT PETS! GUARANTEED LIVE DELIVERY!

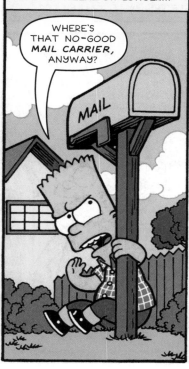

*"TIME AFTER TIME, BARTLEBY WOULD SAVE UP SO HE COULD ORDER HIMSELF A NEW LITTLE FRIEND. HE'D EAGERLY WAIT FOR SIX WEEKS OR LONGER..."*

WHERE'S THAT NO-GOOD *MAIL CARRIER*, ANYWAY?

MAIL

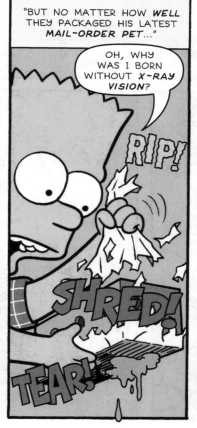

*"BUT NO MATTER HOW WELL THEY PACKAGED HIS LATEST MAIL-ORDER PET..."*

OH, WHY WAS I BORN WITHOUT *X-RAY* VISION?

RIP!

SHRED!

TEAR!

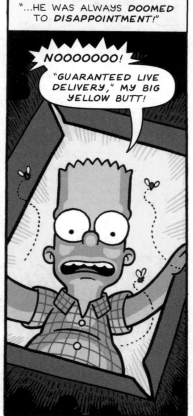

*"...HE WAS ALWAYS DOOMED TO DISAPPOINTMENT!"*

NOOOOOOO!

*"GUARANTEED LIVE DELIVERY,"* MY BIG YELLOW BUTT!

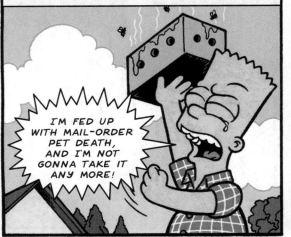

"ONE DAY, AFTER RECEIVING A PARTICULARLY RIPE *DECEASED CHIHUAHUA* IN THE MAIL, BARTLEBY'S MIND FINALLY *SNAPPED!*"

I'M FED UP WITH MAIL-ORDER PET DEATH, AND I'M NOT GONNA TAKE IT ANY MORE!

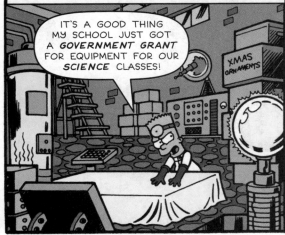

"BEFORE LONG, BARTLEBY HAD SCROUNGED TOGETHER ENOUGH *SCIENTIFIC STUFF* TO OUTFIT HIS VERY OWN *LABORATORY!*"

IT'S A GOOD THING MY SCHOOL JUST GOT A *GOVERNMENT GRANT* FOR EQUIPMENT FOR OUR *SCIENCE* CLASSES!

XMAS ORNAMENTS

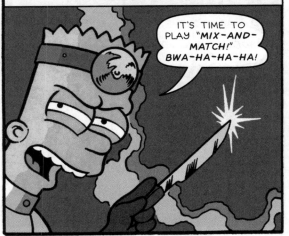

"YOU SEE, BARTLEBY WAS *DETERMINED* TO BRING BACK ALL OF THOSE MAIL-ORDER PETS WHO ARRIVED IN, ER, LESS-THAN-MINT CONDITION!"

IT'S TIME TO PLAY "MIX-AND-MATCH!" BWA-HA-HA-HA!

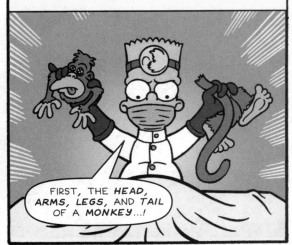

"BARTLEBY TOOK THE *LEFTOVER PARTS* AND BEGAN TO *STITCH* THEM TOGETHER!"

FIRST, THE *HEAD, ARMS, LEGS,* AND *TAIL* OF A *MONKEY*...!

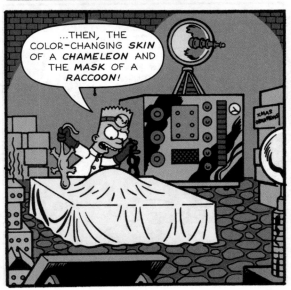

...THEN, THE COLOR-CHANGING *SKIN* OF A *CHAMELEON* AND THE *MASK* OF A *RACCOON!*

XMAS ORNAMENTS

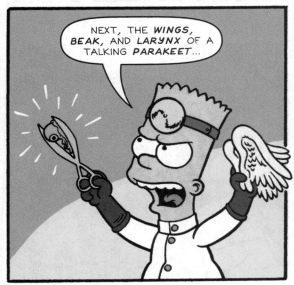

NEXT, THE *WINGS, BEAK,* AND *LARYNX* OF A TALKING *PARAKEET*...

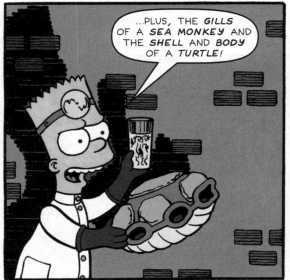

...PLUS, THE *GILLS* OF A *SEA MONKEY* AND THE *SHELL* AND *BODY* OF A *TURTLE!*

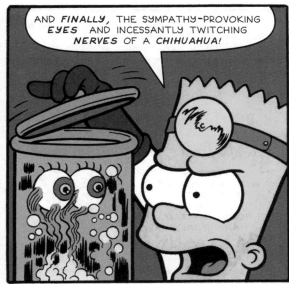

AND *FINALLY*, THE SYMPATHY-PROVOKING *EYES* AND INCESSANTLY TWITCHING *NERVES* OF A *CHIHUAHUA!*

"AT LONG LAST, BARTLEBY FINISHED PIECING TOGETHER HIS MULTI-SPECIES CREATURE, BUT HE HAD YET TO GIVE IT THE SPARK OF *LIFE!*"

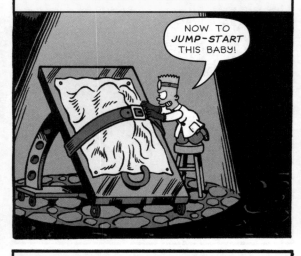

NOW TO *JUMP-START* THIS BABY!

"FORTUNATELY, BARTLEBY HAD THE RIGHT *RADIOACTIVE RESOURCES* TO PROPERLY PERFORM HIS UNHOLY *TASK!*"

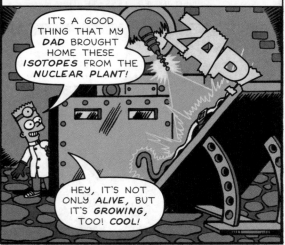

IT'S A GOOD THING THAT MY *DAD* BROUGHT HOME THESE *ISOTOPES* FROM THE *NUCLEAR PLANT!*

HEY, IT'S NOT ONLY *ALIVE*, BUT IT'S *GROWING*, TOO! *COOL!*

ZAP

"BARTLEBY'S MONSTROUS *MEGA-PET* CONTINUED TO GROW TO A SIZE THAT HIS BASEMENT COULDN'T *CONTAIN!*"

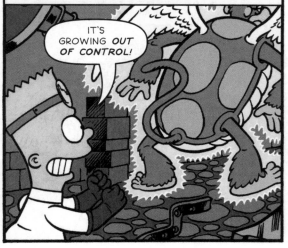

IT'S GROWING *OUT OF CONTROL!*

"BUT ONCE BARTLEBY'S CREATION WAS FREE, IT COULD FINALLY CARRY OUT ITS MASTER'S FIENDISH *ORDERS!*"

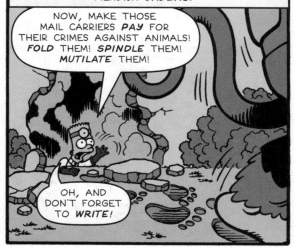

NOW, MAKE THOSE MAIL CARRIERS *PAY* FOR THEIR CRIMES AGAINST ANIMALS! *FOLD* THEM! *SPINDLE* THEM! *MUTILATE* THEM!

OH, AND DON'T FORGET TO *WRITE!*

"BARTLEBY'S BIG OL' BEAST WAS SURPRISINGLY OBEDIENT! IT HEADED STRAIGHT FOR THE TOWN'S MAIN POST OFFICE WITH MAYHEM ON ITS MIND!"
YAARRGHH!
SPRINGFIELD POST OFFICE
ACME
KIRBY MOVERS
EGAD! THAT CREATURE LOOKS AS IF THE MAIL-ORDER PET CATALOG EXPLODED!
THAT'S THE SECOND BIGGEST MONSTER I'VE EVER SEEN!
AND THE THIRD UGLIEST!
AND UNFORTUNATELY, :CHOKE!: THE FIRST SMELLIEST!

"AND AFTER IT *STOMPED* ON THE MAIN POST OFFICE, THAT MONSTER WENT *NUTZOID*, WRECKING THE REST OF THE TOWN! ITS *MONKEY PARTS* LOVED TO PLAY MEAN *TRICKS* ON PEOPLE!"

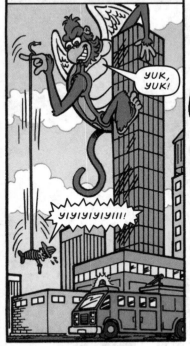

YUK, YUK!

YIYIYIYIYIYI!!!

"ITS *PARAKEET PARTS* LET EVERYONE KNOW WHAT WAS ON ITS MIND! AND REMEMBER, IT WAS RAISED BY A *SAILOR!*"

POLLY WANTS FIVE @#$%&$ TONS OF CRACKERS!

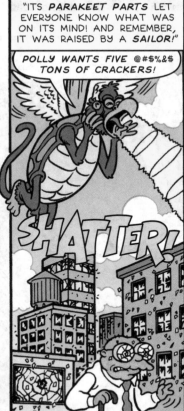

SHATTER!

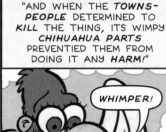

"BUT AT THE SAME TIME, ITS *SEA MONKEY* AND *TURTLE* PARTS CRAVED *SEAFOOD!*"

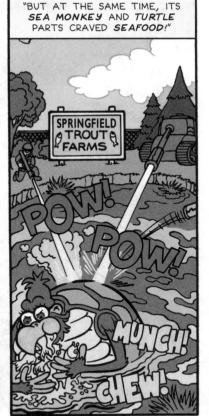

SPRINGFIELD TROUT FARMS

POW!

POW!

MUNCH!

CHEW!

"WHEN THE *POLICE* FINALLY CORNERED BARTLEBY'S MONSTER, ITS *CHAMELEON PARTS* MADE IT APPEAR TO *VANISH* BY USING ITS SKIN TO *CAMOUFLAGE* ITSELF!"

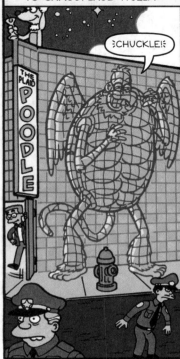

:CHUCKLE!:

THE PLAID POODLE

"AND WHEN THE *TOWNS-PEOPLE* DETERMINED TO *KILL* THE THING, ITS WIMPY *CHIHUAHUA PARTS* PREVENTED THEM FROM DOING IT ANY *HARM!*"

WHIMPER!

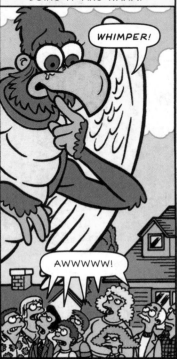

AWWWWW!

BUT THERE *WAS* ONE PERSON WHO THOUGHT SHE COULD *STOP* BARTLEBY'S BEHEMOTH DEAD IN ITS TRACKS! LET'S CALL HER... HMM...HOW ABOUT..."LISA"?

LIKE YOUR *SISTER* LISA?

*NO!* SHE'S NOT AT *ALL* LIKE LISA! SHE WAS BARTLEBY'S *STEP*SISTER!

LET'S CALL HER "*LESSA*"!

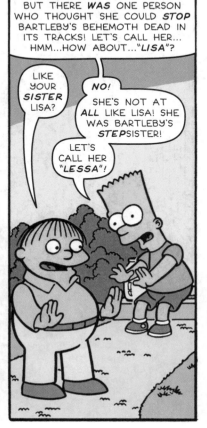

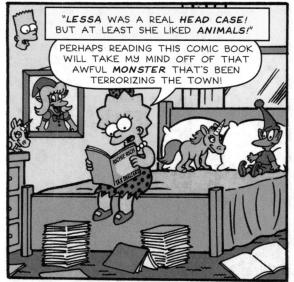

"*LESSA* WAS A REAL *HEAD CASE!* BUT AT LEAST SHE LIKED *ANIMALS!*"

PERHAPS READING THIS COMIC BOOK WILL TAKE MY MIND OFF OF THAT AWFUL *MONSTER* THAT'S BEEN TERRORIZING THE TOWN!

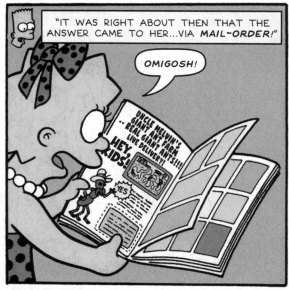

"IT WAS RIGHT ABOUT THEN THAT THE ANSWER CAME TO HER...VIA *MAIL-ORDER!*"

OMIGOSH!

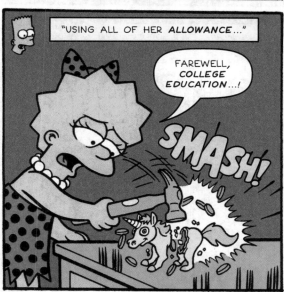

"USING ALL OF HER *ALLOWANCE*..."

FAREWELL, *COLLEGE EDUCATION*...!

SMASH!

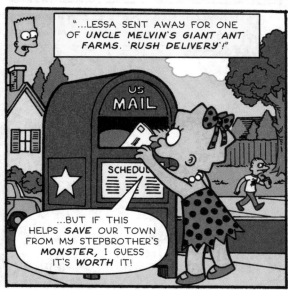

"...LESSA SENT AWAY FOR ONE OF *UNCLE MELVIN'S GIANT ANT FARMS.* 'RUSH DELIVERY'!"

US MAIL

...BUT IF THIS HELPS *SAVE* OUR TOWN FROM MY STEPBROTHER'S *MONSTER*, I GUESS IT'S *WORTH* IT!

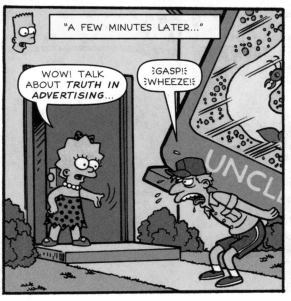

"A FEW MINUTES LATER..."

WOW! TALK ABOUT *TRUTH IN ADVERTISING*...

¦GASP!¦ ¦WHEEZE!¦

UNCL

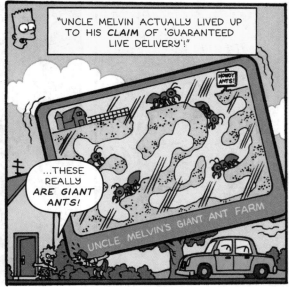

"UNCLE MELVIN ACTUALLY LIVED UP TO HIS *CLAIM* OF 'GUARANTEED LIVE DELIVERY'!"

...THESE REALLY *ARE GIANT ANTS!*

UNCLE MELVIN'S GIANT ANT FARM

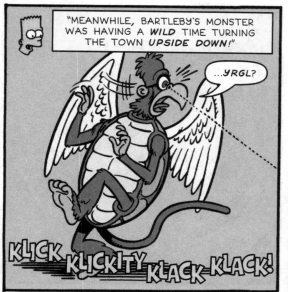

"MEANWHILE, BARTLEBY'S MONSTER WAS HAVING A *WILD* TIME TURNING THE TOWN *UPSIDE DOWN!*"

...YRGL?

KLICK KLICKITY KLACK KLACK!

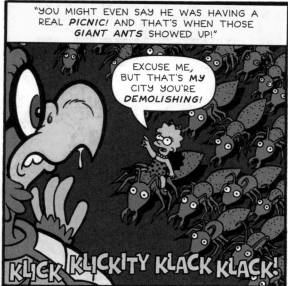

"YOU MIGHT EVEN SAY HE WAS HAVING A REAL *PICNIC!* AND THAT'S WHEN THOSE *GIANT ANTS* SHOWED UP!"

EXCUSE ME, BUT THAT'S *MY* CITY YOU'RE *DEMOLISHING!*

KLICK KLICKITY KLACK KLACK!

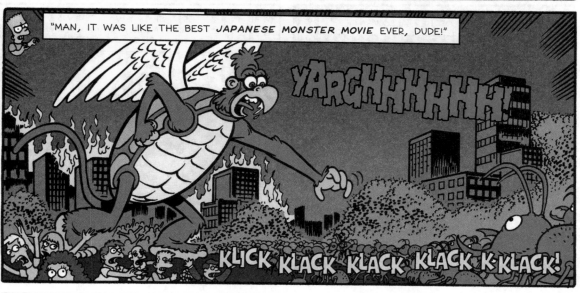

"MAN, IT WAS LIKE THE BEST *JAPANESE MONSTER MOVIE* EVER, DUDE!"

YARGHHHHHH!

KLICK KLACK KLACK KLACK K-KLACK!

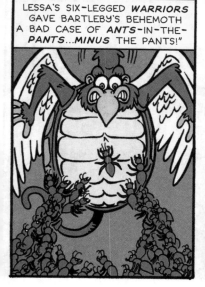

LESSA'S SIX-LEGGED *WARRIORS* GAVE BARTLEBY'S BEHEMOTH A BAD CASE OF *ANTS*-IN-THE-*PANTS...MINUS* THE PANTS!

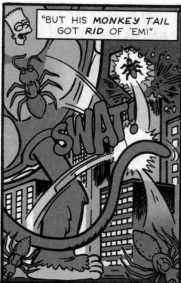

"BUT HIS *MONKEY TAIL* GOT *RID* OF 'EM!"

SWAT!

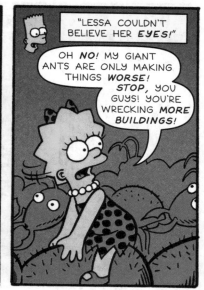

"LESSA COULDN'T BELIEVE HER *EYES!*"

OH *NO!* MY GIANT ANTS ARE ONLY MAKING THINGS *WORSE! STOP,* YOU GUYS! YOU'RE WRECKING *MORE* BUILDINGS!

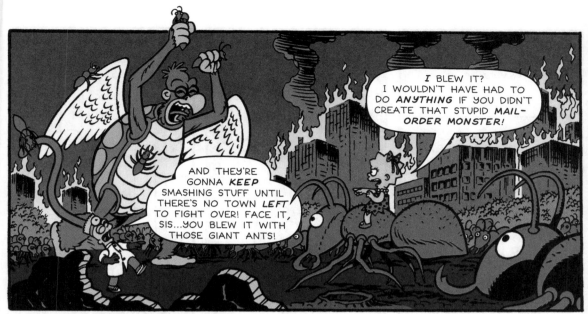

AND THEY'RE GONNA *KEEP* SMASHING STUFF UNTIL THERE'S NO TOWN *LEFT* TO FIGHT OVER! FACE IT, SIS...YOU BLEW IT WITH THOSE GIANT ANTS!

*I* BLEW IT? I WOULDN'T HAVE HAD TO DO *ANYTHING* IF YOU DIDN'T CREATE THAT STUPID *MAIL-ORDER MONSTER!*

"SUDDENLY, BARTLEBY'S BRILLIANTLY DEMENTED *BRAIN* CONCOCTED A GREAT *IDEA!*"

HEY! THAT'S *IT!*

*SNAP!*

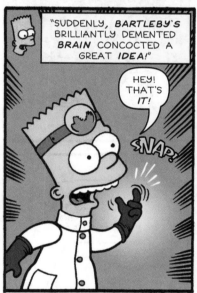

"THEY PAID A LITTLE *VISIT* TO WHAT WAS *LEFT* OF THE TOWN'S *POST OFFICE...*"

SO YOU SEE, SIR, I FIGURE THAT IF THE *POSTAL SERVICE* CAN *CROAK* MY MAIL-ORDER *PETS* WITHOUT EVEN *TRYING...*

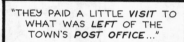

...YOU OUGHT TO BE ABLE TO *REALLY TRASH* GIANT *MONSTERS* IF YOU JUST PUT YOUR *MINDS* TO IT.

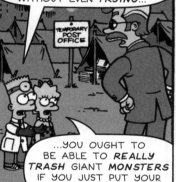

¿SPUTTER!¿ WELL, SINCE YOU PUT THINGS *THAT* WAY, I THINK WE MIGHT BE ABLE TO *ASSIST* YOU...BY DOING WHAT WE DO *BEST!*

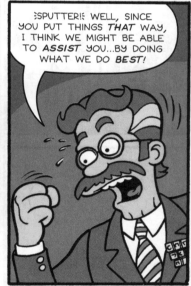

FOLD! SPINDLE! MUTILATE!

NOW *THAT'S* WHAT I CALL *POSTAL!*

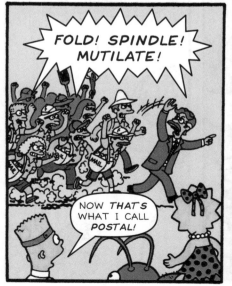

"FORTUNATELY, THAT POSTMASTER AND HIS CREW REALLY *LIVED UP* TO THEIR *REPUTATION!*"

YARRGHH?!?

FOLD!

SPINDLE!

MUTILATE!

CANCEL!

RETURN TO SENDER!

*KLACK? KLICK?*

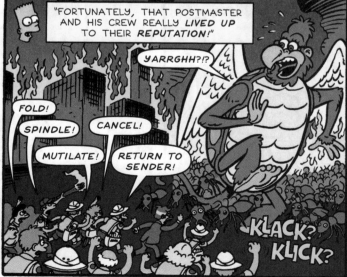

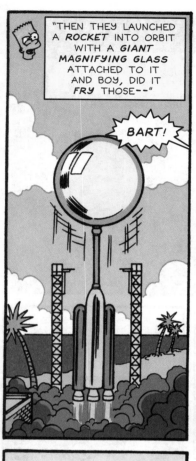

"THEN THEY LAUNCHED A *ROCKET* INTO ORBIT WITH A *GIANT MAGNIFYING GLASS* ATTACHED TO IT AND BOY, DID IT *FRY* THOSE--"

BART!

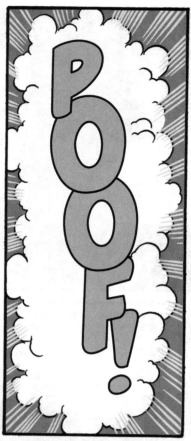

POOF!

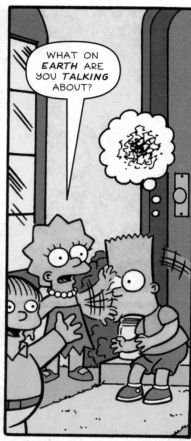

WHAT ON *EARTH* ARE YOU *TALKING* ABOUT?

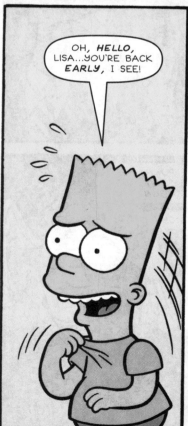

OH, *HELLO*, LISA...YOU'RE BACK *EARLY*, I SEE!

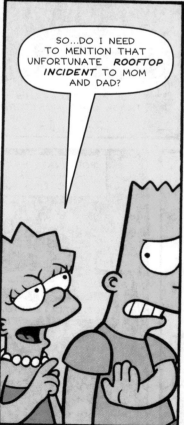

SO...DO I NEED TO MENTION THAT UNFORTUNATE *ROOFTOP INCIDENT* TO MOM AND DAD?

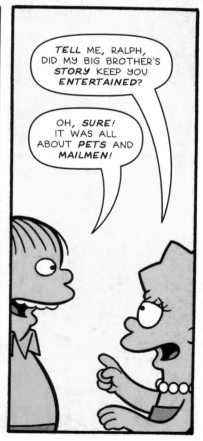

*TELL* ME, RALPH, DID MY BIG BROTHER'S *STORY* KEEP YOU *ENTERTAINED*?

OH, *SURE!* IT WAS ALL ABOUT *PETS* AND *MAILMEN!*

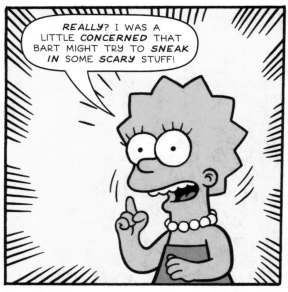

REALLY? I WAS A LITTLE *CONCERNED* THAT BART MIGHT TRY TO *SNEAK IN* SOME *SCARY* STUFF!

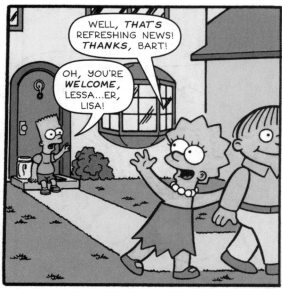

WELL, *THAT'S* REFRESHING NEWS! *THANKS*, BART!

OH, YOU'RE *WELCOME*, LESSA...ER, LISA!

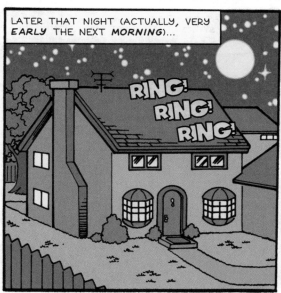

LATER THAT NIGHT (ACTUALLY, VERY *EARLY* THE NEXT *MORNING*)...

RING! RING! RING!

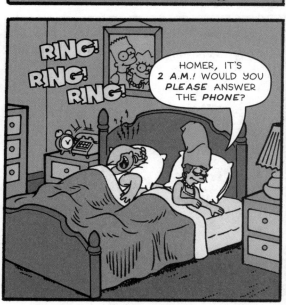

RING! RING! RING!

HOMER, IT'S *2 A.M.!* WOULD YOU *PLEASE* ANSWER THE *PHONE*?

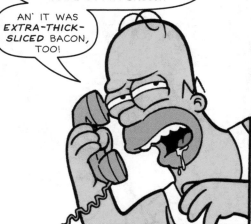

THIS BETTER BE *GOOD*, BUDDY! YOU JUST WOKE ME UP FROM A *DREAM* WHERE OUR DOG, *SANTA'S LITTLE HELPER*, WAS MADE OUTTA *BACON*!

AN' IT WAS *EXTRA-THICK-SLICED* BACON, TOO!

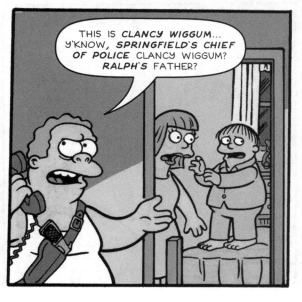

THIS IS *CLANCY WIGGUM*... Y'KNOW, *SPRINGFIELD'S CHIEF OF POLICE* CLANCY WIGGUM? *RALPH'S* FATHER?

WELL, WE'RE HAVING ONE HECK OF A TIME GETTING RALPHIE BACK TO SLEEP!
HE KEEPS HAVING NIGHTMARES ABOUT GIANT MONSTERS.
YEAH, SO WHAT DO YOUR BOY'S NIGHTMARES HAVE TO DO WITH ME?
HE SAYS IT'S ALL BECAUSE OF SOME CRAZY STORY THAT BART TOLD HIM TODAY!
AW C'MON, HONEY...PLEASE GO BACK TO SLEEP!
NO, MAMA, NO! THE GIANT MONKEY-CHAMELEON-RACCOON-PARAKEET-SEA MONKEY-TURTLE-CHIHUAHUA WILL GOBBLE ME UP IF I'M ASLEEP...!
YEAH, THAT SOUNDS LIKE THE KIND OF STORY THAT BART LIKES TO TELL, ALL RIGHT...
...AND THE GIANT ANTS WILL EAT MY LEFTOVERS!
UH...DID THAT KID JUST SAY "LEFTOVERS"?
:SIGH!: OH, HOMIE...
SORRY, CHIEF, BUT I'VE GOT A SUDDEN DATE WITH A LATE-NIGHT SNACK!
HELLO?... HELLO?...
THE END

# BART & LISA SIMPSON in
# PLANET OF THE PLANTS

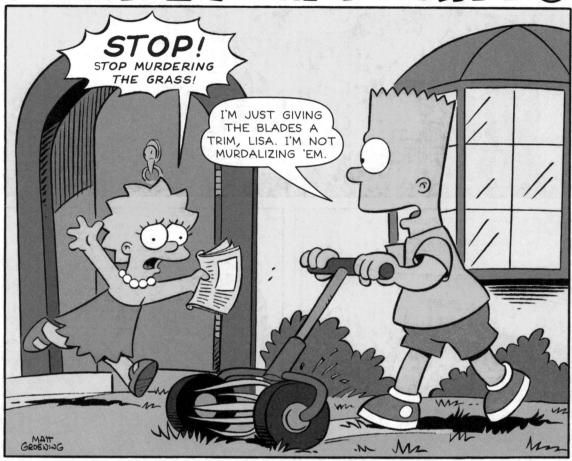

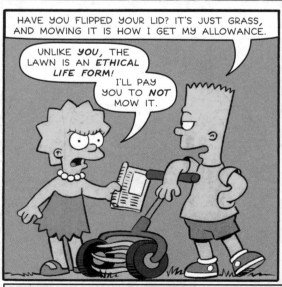

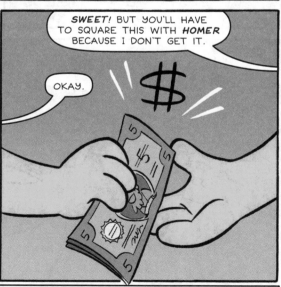

CAROL LAY
STORY & ART

NATHAN HAMILL
COLORS

KAREN BATES
LETTERS

BILL MORRISON
EDITOR

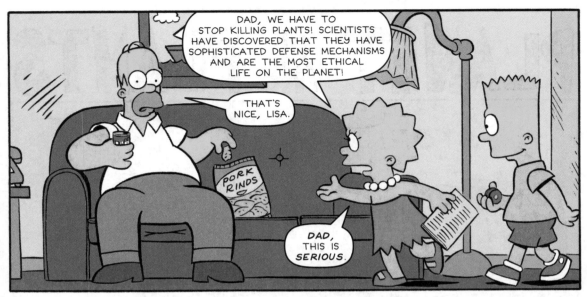

DAD, WE HAVE TO STOP KILLING PLANTS! SCIENTISTS HAVE DISCOVERED THAT THEY HAVE SOPHISTICATED DEFENSE MECHANISMS AND ARE THE MOST ETHICAL LIFE ON THE PLANET!

THAT'S NICE, LISA.

PORK RINDS

DAD, THIS IS *SERIOUS*.

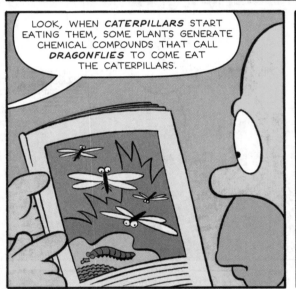

LOOK, WHEN *CATERPILLARS* START EATING THEM, SOME PLANTS GENERATE CHEMICAL COMPOUNDS THAT CALL *DRAGONFLIES* TO COME EAT THE CATERPILLARS.

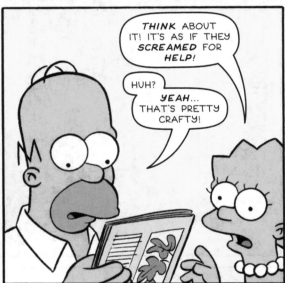

*THINK* ABOUT IT! IT'S AS IF THEY *SCREAMED* FOR *HELP*!

HUH?

*YEAH...* THAT'S PRETTY CRAFTY!

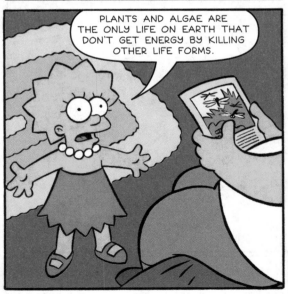

PLANTS AND ALGAE ARE THE ONLY LIFE ON EARTH THAT DON'T GET ENERGY BY KILLING OTHER LIFE FORMS.

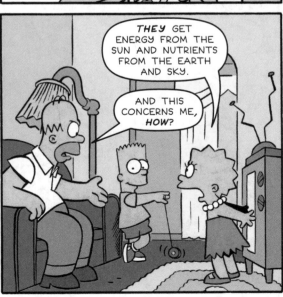

*THEY* GET ENERGY FROM THE SUN AND NUTRIENTS FROM THE EARTH AND SKY.

AND THIS CONCERNS ME, *HOW*?

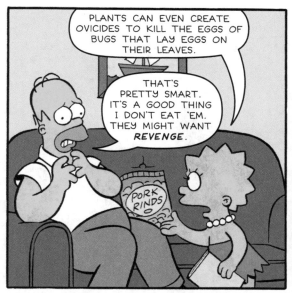

PLANTS CAN EVEN CREATE OVICIDES TO KILL THE EGGS OF BUGS THAT LAY EGGS ON THEIR LEAVES.

THAT'S PRETTY SMART. IT'S A GOOD THING I DON'T EAT 'EM. THEY MIGHT WANT *REVENGE*.

PORK RINDS

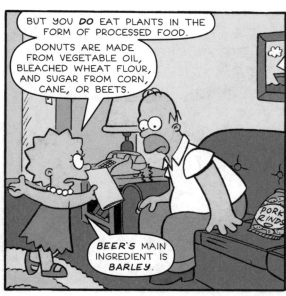

BUT YOU *DO* EAT PLANTS IN THE FORM OF PROCESSED FOOD.

DONUTS ARE MADE FROM VEGETABLE OIL, BLEACHED WHEAT FLOUR, AND SUGAR FROM CORN, CANE, OR BEETS.

*BEER'S* MAIN INGREDIENT IS *BARLEY*.

PORK RINDS

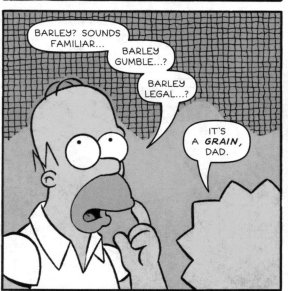

BARLEY? SOUNDS FAMILIAR...

BARLEY GUMBLE...?

BARLEY LEGAL...?

IT'S A *GRAIN*, DAD.

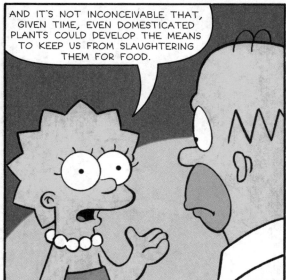

AND IT'S NOT INCONCEIVABLE THAT, GIVEN TIME, EVEN DOMESTICATED PLANTS COULD DEVELOP THE MEANS TO KEEP US FROM SLAUGHTERING THEM FOR FOOD.

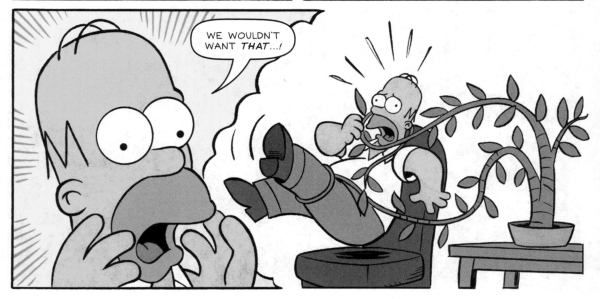

WE WOULDN'T WANT *THAT*...!

LISA, I PROMISE TO GIVE UP EATING ALL PLANTS, EVEN DONUTS AND BEER!
FROM NOW ON I'LL JUST EAT MEAT AND MAYBE THE FRUIT THAT PLANTS HAVE ALREADY THROWN OUT.
BUT, DAD, CATTLE EAT GRASSES AND GRAIN.
AND FRUIT TREES NEED TO PROPAGATE, TOO! FRUITS CONTAIN THE SEEDS THAT ENSURE CONTINUATION OF THE SPECIES, SO EATING FRUIT IS LIKE EATING LITTLE TREE BABIES.
LITTLE TREE BABIES?!
OH MY LORD, I'VE BEEN EATING TREE BABIES!
EEEK!
IT WANTS TO KILL ME!
KUDOS, LIS. WAY TO FREAK OUT HOMER.

SO WHAT THE HECK WILL YOU EAT? YOU ALREADY DON'T EAT ANYTHING THAT SWIMS, FLIES, OR GROWS HAIR.
THAT'S A GOOD QUESTION.
OH, WHY CAN'T I PERFORM PHOTOSYNTHESIS LIKE PLANTS DO?
THERE'S SO MUCH TO LEARN FROM PLANTS. THEY ARE THE MOST ETHICAL LIFE FORM ON THE PLANET.
BLINK!
WHAT DO ETHICS HAVE TO DO WITH IT? HUMANS INVENTED THEM. PLANTS JUST DO WHAT THEY CAN TO SURVIVE.
HOW CAN YOU BE SO CALLOUS? LOOK AT THIS INNOCENT LIFE FORM. IT COULD NEVER HURT EVEN A FLY.
NO, BUT IT'S GOT A REALLY COOL COUSIN THAT COULD.
I DON'T CARE WHAT YOU SAY...I PLEDGE MY RESPECT TO THIS PLANT AND ALL ITS BRETHREN.
SUIT YOURSELF.
KIDS! TIME FOR DINNER!

OHHH... PLANTS SAD. PLANTS MIGHT GET ANGRY.
YES, IT IS SAD THAT WE TOOK THEIR LIVES.
WHAT ARE YOU TALKING ABOUT?
LISA THINKS EATING PLANTS IS MURDER NOW. I AGREE. I REFUSE TO EAT THESE VEGETABLES.
I SAY WE TAKE THEM OUTSIDE AND GIVE THEM A PROPER BURIAL.
YES, THEN THEY WOULD RETURN NUTRIENTS TO THE SOIL AND PASS THEM ON TO OTHER PLANTS. THEY WON'T HAVE DIED IN VAIN.
LISA, HONEY, THERE'S NOTHING WRONG WITH EATING **PLANTS**.

IT'S WONDERFUL THAT YOU RESPECT AND CARE FOR MOTHER NATURE AND ALL HER CHILDREN, INCLUDING THE FLORA.
BUT PEOPLE ARE A PART OF THE CIRCLE OF LIFE, TOO. WE NEED PLANTS FOR OXYGEN AND ENERGY SO WE CAN LIVE.
BUT DON'T PLANTS HAVE AS MUCH RIGHT TO LIVE AS WE DO?
HEY, IF PLANTS COULD LEARN TO RUN, THEY'D INCREASE THEIR CHANCES OF SURVIVAL.
THAT'S NOT IMPOSSIBLE, YOU KNOW. ANIMALS EVOLVED IN THE SEA AND THEN DEVELOPED LEGS WHEN THEY VENTURED ONTO LAND.
HMM... MAYBE HELPING **PLANTS GROW LEGS** WILL BE MY NEXT SCIENCE PROJECT.
**THEN** WHAT?! WILL YOU HELP THEM GROW **ARMS** SO THEY CAN HACK US TO DEATH LIKE WE'VE BEEN DOING TO THEM?!
HOMER, DON'T BE RIDICULOUS. PLANTS CAN'T BUY MACHETES... THEY DON'T HAVE ANY MONEY.
PLEASE FORGIVE US.
PLEASE DON'T HURT ME!

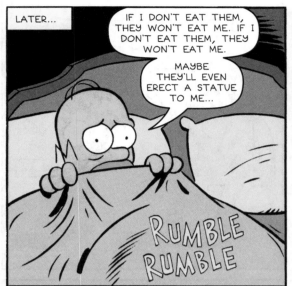

LATER...

IF I DON'T EAT THEM, THEY WON'T EAT ME. IF I DON'T EAT THEM, THEY WON'T EAT ME.

MAYBE THEY'LL EVEN ERECT A STATUE TO ME...

RUMBLE RUMBLE

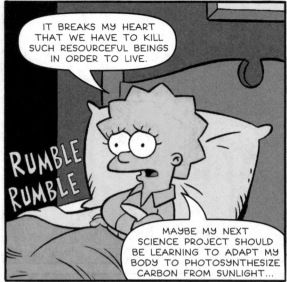

IT BREAKS MY HEART THAT WE HAVE TO KILL SUCH RESOURCEFUL BEINGS IN ORDER TO LIVE.

RUMBLE RUMBLE

MAYBE MY NEXT SCIENCE PROJECT SHOULD BE LEARNING TO ADAPT MY BODY TO PHOTOSYNTHESIZE CARBON FROM SUNLIGHT...

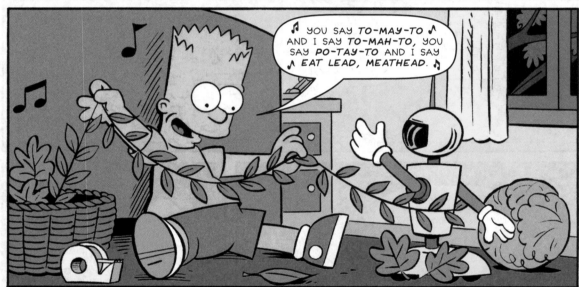

♪ YOU SAY *TO-MAY-TO* ♪ AND I SAY *TO-MAH-TO*, YOU SAY *PO-TAY-TO* AND I SAY ♪ *EAT LEAD, MEATHEAD.* ♪

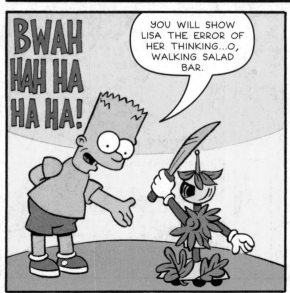

BWAH HAH HA HA HA!

YOU WILL SHOW LISA THE ERROR OF HER THINKING...O, WALKING SALAD BAR.

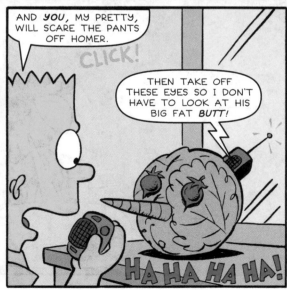

AND *YOU*, MY PRETTY, WILL SCARE THE PANTS OFF HOMER.

CLICK!

THEN TAKE OFF THESE EYES SO I DON'T HAVE TO LOOK AT HIS BIG FAT *BUTT*!

HA HA HA HA!

IF ONLY PLANTS COULD WALK...
YEAH... JUST LIKE ...THAT...
RUMBLE GURGLE RUMBLE
NOW YOU ARE FREE! FREE TO LIVE WITHOUT FEARING OUR BLADES!
AND NOW YOU HAVE SPEECH! TEACH US HUMANS TO BE MORE LIKE YOU!
LI-SA! LI-SA! LI-SA!
THANK YOU, MS. LISA, FOR HELPING US ADVANCE OUR CIVILIZATION!
LI-SA!
LET US PRAISE LISA!
AND NOW THAT HUMANS HAVE JOINED THE PLANT WORLD IN ETHICAL LIVING, THE EARTH IS SAFE, AND WAR AND HUNGER ARE BUT DISTANT MEMORIES.
ALL HAIL QUEEN LISA!

SO HUNGRY... MUST NOT UPSET... PLANTS...
WE SHALL OVERRUN!
ACKK!
GIVE IT UP, HOMER...YOUR CHEMICAL COMPOSITION WILL MAKE YOU THE *BEST FERTILIZER EVER!*

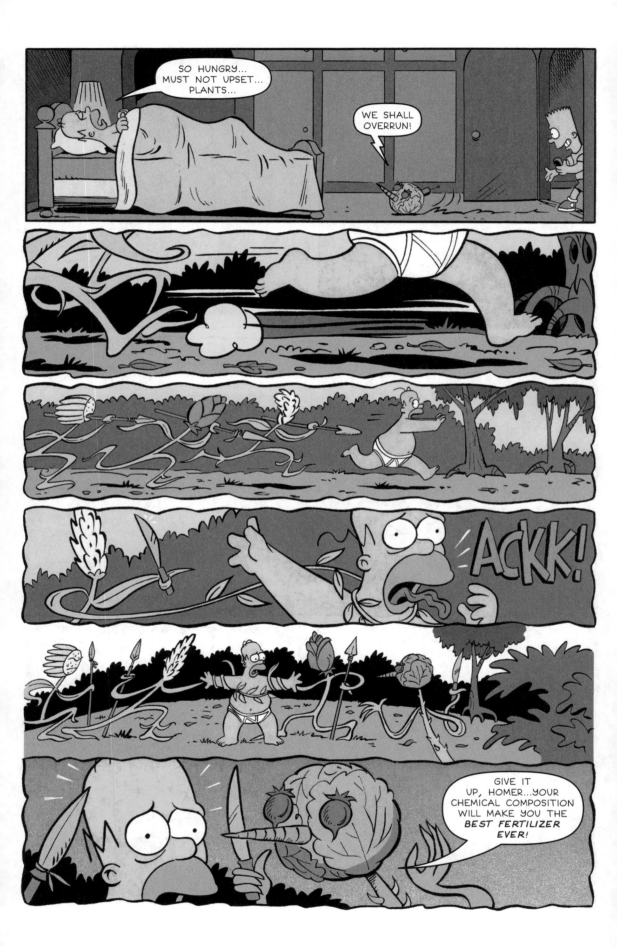

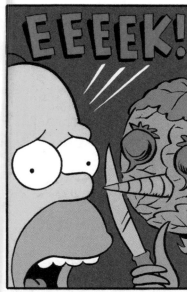

EEEEK!

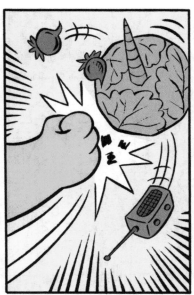

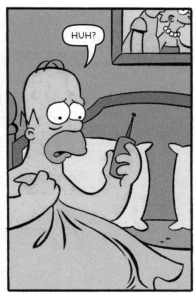

HUH?

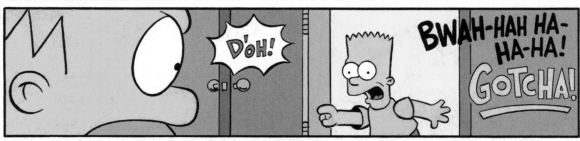

D'OH!

BWAH-HAH HA-HA-HA!

GOTCHA!

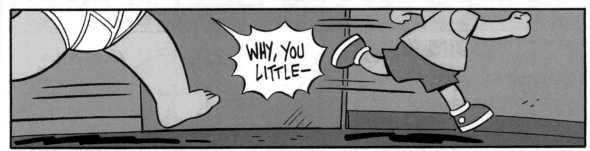

WHY, YOU LITTLE—

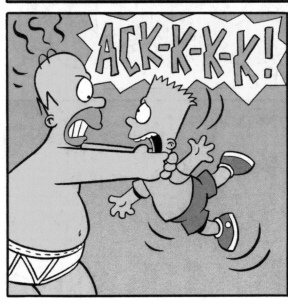

ACK-K-K-K!

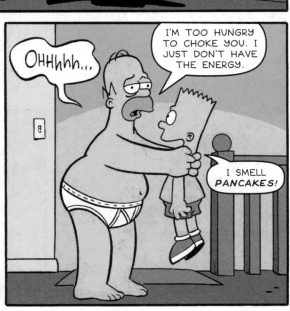

OHHHHH...

I'M TOO HUNGRY TO CHOKE YOU. I JUST DON'T HAVE THE ENERGY.

I SMELL PANCAKES!

COME AND GET IT! BUCKWHEAT PANCAKES WITH BUTTER AND MAPLE SYRUP!
MOANNN! I'M SO *HUNGRY*.
ZOOM!!
BUT EATING BUCKWHEAT IS LIKE EATING THE HEADS OF PLANTS. AND SYRUP IS LIKE THE BLOOD OF TREES!
THIS IS *SO WRONG!*
Gobble
CHOMP
SCARF
SLURP
CHEW
IT'S *US* OR *THEM*.
WE MUST EAT THEM BEFORE THEY GET *TOO STRONG!*
BURP!
Gobble
SNORT
SCARF
AND LISA'S GOT TO EAT BEFORE SHE GETS TOO *WEAK!*
RUMBLE
RUMBLE

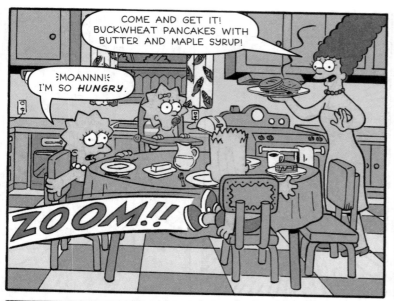

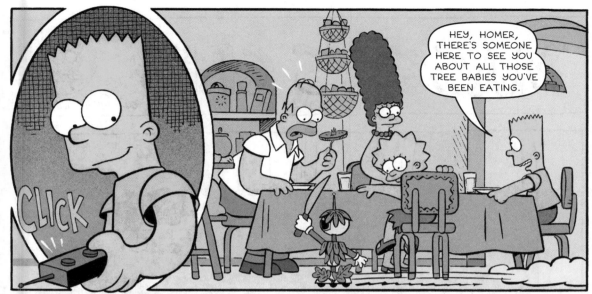

HEY, HOMER, THERE'S SOMEONE HERE TO SEE YOU ABOUT ALL THOSE TREE BABIES YOU'VE BEEN EATING.

CLICK

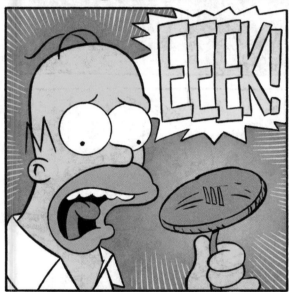

EEEK!

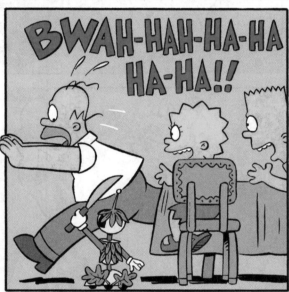

BWAH-HAH-HA-HA HA-HA!!

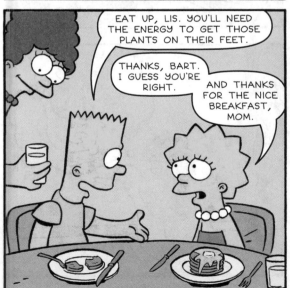

EAT UP, LIS. YOU'LL NEED THE ENERGY TO GET THOSE PLANTS ON THEIR FEET.

THANKS, BART. I GUESS YOU'RE RIGHT.

AND THANKS FOR THE NICE BREAKFAST, MOM.

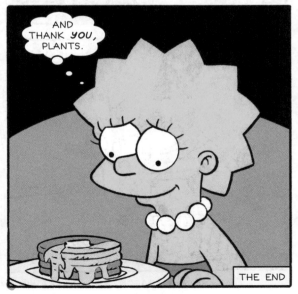

AND THANK *YOU*, PLANTS.

THE END

# MAGGIE'S CRIB

by ARAGONÉS

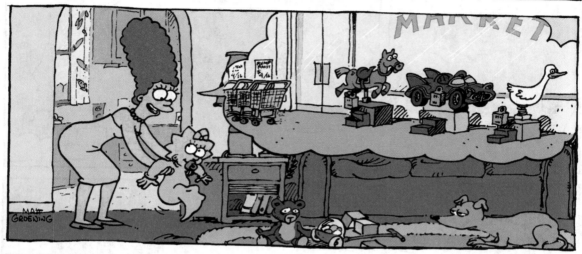

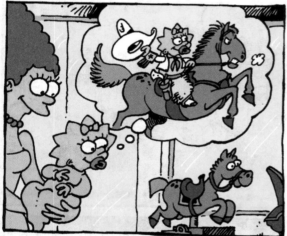

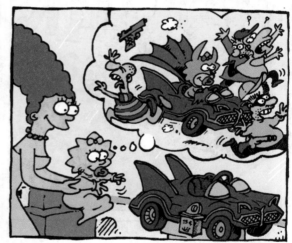

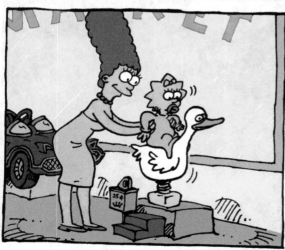

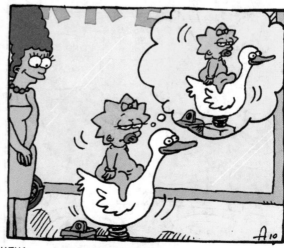

**SERGIO ARAGONÉS**
STORY & ART

**ART VILLANUEVA**
COLORS

**BILL MORRISON**
EDITOR

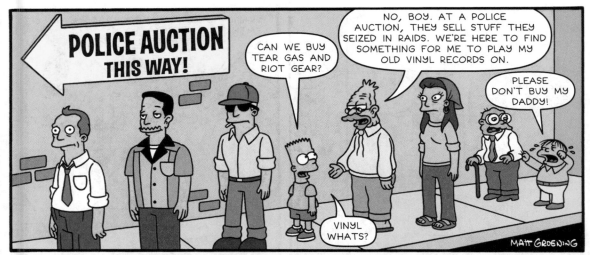

POLICE AUCTION THIS WAY!

CAN WE BUY TEAR GAS AND RIOT GEAR?

NO, BOY. AT A POLICE AUCTION, THEY SELL STUFF THEY SEIZED IN RAIDS. WE'RE HERE TO FIND SOMETHING FOR ME TO PLAY MY OLD VINYL RECORDS ON.

PLEASE DON'T BUY MY DADDY!

VINYL WHATS?

MATT GROENING

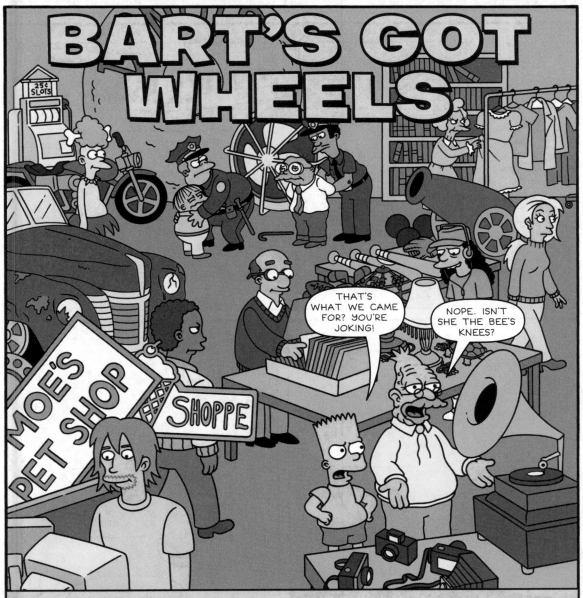

# BART'S GOT WHEELS

25¢ SLOTS

MOE'S PET SHOP

SHOPPE

THAT'S WHAT WE CAME FOR? YOU'RE JOKING!

NOPE. ISN'T SHE THE BEE'S KNEES?

JAMES W. BATES
SCRIPT

NINA MATSUMOTO
PENCILS

MIKE ROTE
INKS

NATHAN HAMILL
COLORS

KAREN BATES
LETTERS

BILL MORRISON
EDITOR

I CAN ALMOST HEAR THE BIG BANDS! IF I COULD AFFORD TO HAVE MY KNEES REPLACED, I'D DO THE LINDY HOP!

I'M GUESSING THIS DOESN'T PLAY MP3s.

GRAMOPHONES PLAY *RECORDS!* THIS ONE...*WOWZA!* LOOK AT *THAT!*

WHAT IS IT GRAM-O-PA?

SHE'S A BEAUT! I *HAVE* TO BUY THIS CAR!

FIND OUT IF THE SQUIRRELS COST EXTRA.

POLICE AUCTION

AS A YOUNG MAN, I HAD A CAR JUST LIKE THIS!

YOU LOOK SO HAPPY.

SHE WAS MY FIRST CAR, AND I LOVED HER.

BUT THIS ONE IS A RUSTY MESS. WHAT ARE YOU GONNA DO WITH IT ANYWAY?

I'M GONNA FIX HER UP RIGHT, SO THAT MY GRANDSON CAN EXPERIENCE THE SAME JOY I FELT!

YOU WANT *ME* TO HAVE A CAR?

IT'LL TAKE A LOT OF WORK, BUT SHE'S WORTH IT. UNLESS YOU'D RATHER HAVE A STATE OF THE ART VICTROLA.

LET'S GO BID BEFORE SOMEONE ELSE TRIES TO BUY MY CAR!

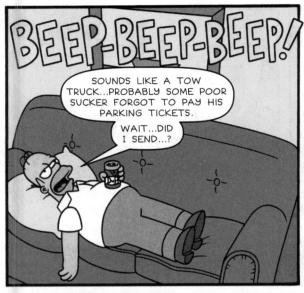

BEEP-BEEP-BEEP!

SOUNDS LIKE A TOW TRUCK...PROBABLY SOME POOR SUCKER FORGOT TO PAY HIS PARKING TICKETS.

WAIT...DID I SEND...?

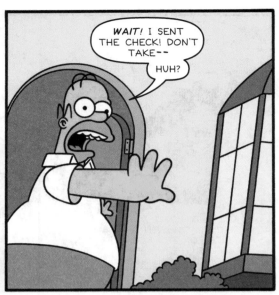

WAIT! I SENT THE CHECK! DON'T TAKE--

HUH?

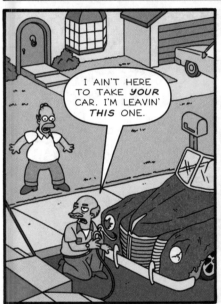

I AIN'T HERE TO TAKE YOUR CAR. I'M LEAVIN' THIS ONE.

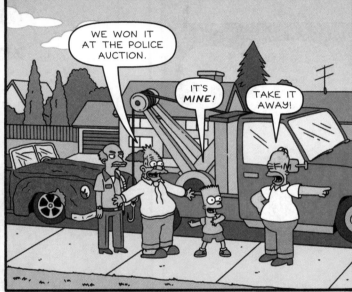

WE WON IT AT THE POLICE AUCTION.

IT'S MINE!

TAKE IT AWAY!

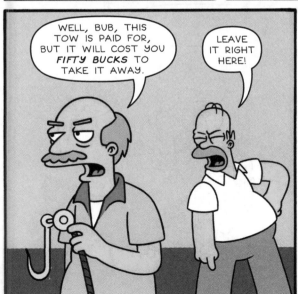

WELL, BUB, THIS TOW IS PAID FOR, BUT IT WILL COST YOU FIFTY BUCKS TO TAKE IT AWAY.

LEAVE IT RIGHT HERE!

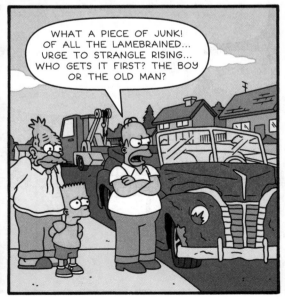

WHAT A PIECE OF JUNK! OF ALL THE LAMEBRAINED... URGE TO STRANGLE RISING... WHO GETS IT FIRST? THE BOY OR THE OLD MAN?

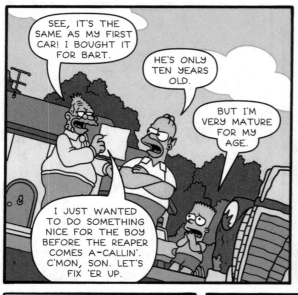

SEE, IT'S THE SAME AS MY FIRST CAR! I BOUGHT IT FOR BART.

HE'S ONLY TEN YEARS OLD.

BUT I'M VERY MATURE FOR MY AGE.

I JUST WANTED TO DO SOMETHING NICE FOR THE BOY BEFORE THE REAPER COMES A-CALLIN'. C'MON, SON. LET'S FIX 'ER UP.

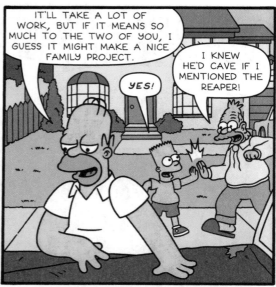

IT'LL TAKE A LOT OF WORK, BUT IF IT MEANS SO MUCH TO THE TWO OF YOU, I GUESS IT MIGHT MAKE A NICE FAMILY PROJECT.

YES!

I KNEW HE'D CAVE IF I MENTIONED THE REAPER!

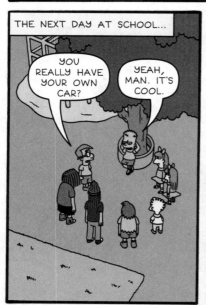

THE NEXT DAY AT SCHOOL...

YOU REALLY HAVE YOUR OWN CAR?

YEAH, MAN. IT'S COOL.

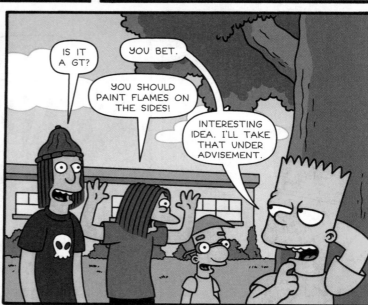

IS IT A GT?

YOU BET.

YOU SHOULD PAINT FLAMES ON THE SIDES!

INTERESTING IDEA. I'LL TAKE THAT UNDER ADVISEMENT.

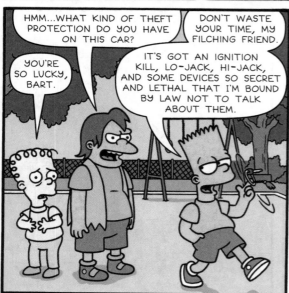

HMM...WHAT KIND OF THEFT PROTECTION DO YOU HAVE ON THIS CAR?

DON'T WASTE YOUR TIME, MY FILCHING FRIEND.

IT'S GOT AN IGNITION KILL, LO-JACK, HI-JACK, AND SOME DEVICES SO SECRET AND LETHAL THAT I'M BOUND BY LAW NOT TO TALK ABOUT THEM.

YOU'RE SO LUCKY, BART.

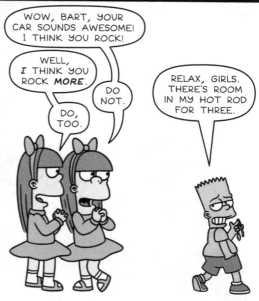

WOW, BART, YOUR CAR SOUNDS AWESOME! I THINK YOU ROCK!

WELL, I THINK YOU ROCK MORE.

DO NOT.

DO, TOO.

RELAX, GIRLS. THERE'S ROOM IN MY HOT ROD FOR THREE.

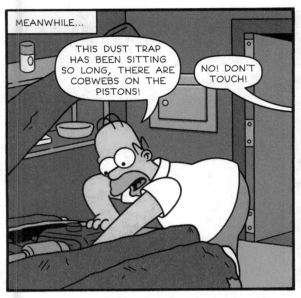

MEANWHILE...

THIS DUST TRAP HAS BEEN SITTING SO LONG, THERE ARE COBWEBS ON THE PISTONS!

NO! DON'T TOUCH!

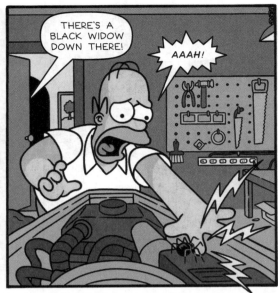

THERE'S A BLACK WIDOW DOWN THERE!

AAAH!

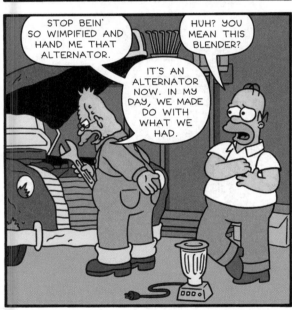

STOP BEIN' SO WIMPIFIED AND HAND ME THAT ALTERNATOR.

HUH? YOU MEAN THIS BLENDER?

IT'S AN ALTERNATOR NOW. IN MY DAY, WE MADE DO WITH WHAT WE HAD.

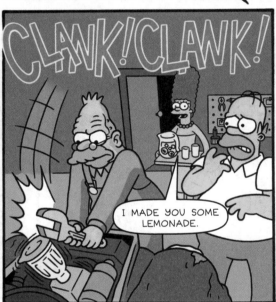

CLANK! CLANK!

I MADE YOU SOME LEMONADE.

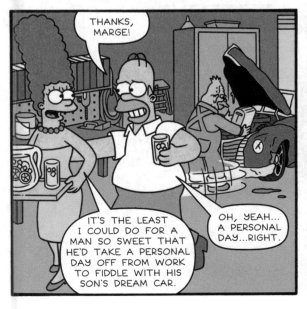

THANKS, MARGE!

IT'S THE LEAST I COULD DO FOR A MAN SO SWEET THAT HE'D TAKE A PERSONAL DAY OFF FROM WORK TO FIDDLE WITH HIS SON'S DREAM CAR.

OH, YEAH... A PERSONAL DAY...RIGHT.

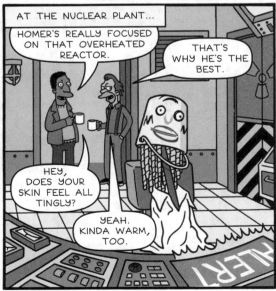

AT THE NUCLEAR PLANT...

HOMER'S REALLY FOCUSED ON THAT OVERHEATED REACTOR.

THAT'S WHY HE'S THE BEST.

HEY, DOES YOUR SKIN FEEL ALL TINGLY?

YEAH. KINDA WARM, TOO.

ALERT

HOLD THAT HOSE TIGHT. I'LL START HER UP.
THAT SPIDER HAD BETTER BE GONE!
CHUG-GHUG-SPUT-SPLASH!
FIRE!! AGH!
MY HAIR! MY LUSH, BEAUTIFUL HAIR IS SINGED!
OH! I KNOW WHAT'S WRONG. I FORGOT THIS ANTI-LEAK AND FIREPROOF TAPE!
HOW'S IT GOING?
GREAT.
COOL!
SNIFF-SNIFF WHAT SMELLS LIKE BURNT PORK RINDS?
GO AHEAD... TURN THE KEY!
CHUG-CHUG-CHUG-VROOOOM!!
AMAZING! IT'S RUNNING.
YES!

I HAVE MY OWN CAR, AND IT RUNS! *I CAN'T BELIEVE IT!*
I CAN'T BELIEVE WE LET YOU DRIVE!
WHAT A PEACH! SHE RUNS JUST LIKE MY FIRST CAR.
YOU KNOW, I BET THE CAR GOES FASTER.
NONSENSE! IT'S BEEN FIFTY YEARS, BUT I KNOW JUST HOW THIS MODEL SHOULD BE DRIVEN.
HEY, SLOWPOKE! YOU DRIVE LIKE AN OLD MAN!
MR. BURNS IS RIGHT, GRAMPA. JASPER JUST PASSED US.
JASPER DOESN'T DRIVE.
NO, HE'S OVER THERE. C'MON! PUT THE PEDAL TO THE METAL.
HERE GOES NOTHIN'.

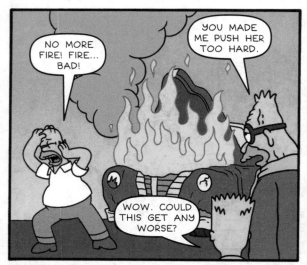

NO MORE FIRE! FIRE... BAD!

YOU MADE ME PUSH HER TOO HARD.

WOW. COULD THIS GET ANY WORSE?

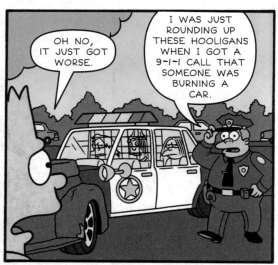

OH NO, IT JUST GOT WORSE.

I WAS JUST ROUNDING UP THESE HOOLIGANS WHEN I GOT A 9-1-1 CALL THAT SOMEONE WAS BURNING A CAR.

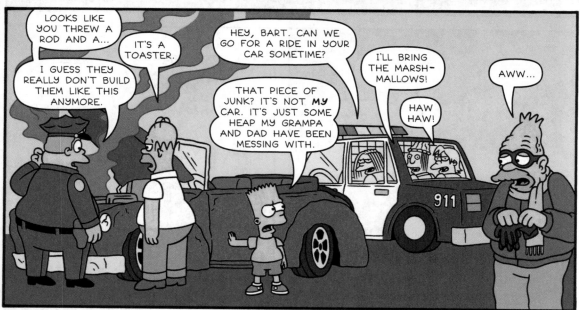

LOOKS LIKE YOU THREW A ROD AND A...

IT'S A TOASTER.

I GUESS THEY REALLY DON'T BUILD THEM LIKE THIS ANYMORE.

HEY, BART. CAN WE GO FOR A RIDE IN YOUR CAR SOMETIME?

THAT PIECE OF JUNK? IT'S NOT **MY** CAR. IT'S JUST SOME HEAP MY GRAMPA AND DAD HAVE BEEN MESSING WITH.

I'LL BRING THE MARSH-MALLOWS!

HAW HAW!

AWW...

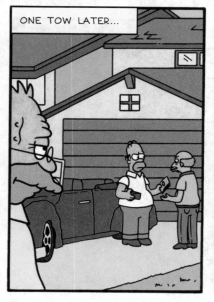

ONE TOW LATER...

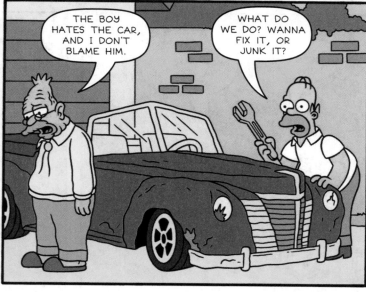

THE BOY HATES THE CAR, AND I DON'T BLAME HIM.

WHAT DO WE DO? WANNA FIX IT, OR JUNK IT?

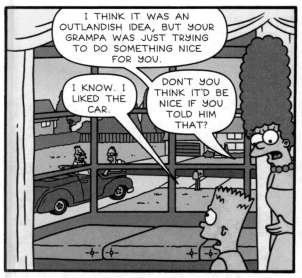

I THINK IT WAS AN OUTLANDISH IDEA, BUT YOUR GRAMPA WAS JUST TRYING TO DO SOMETHING NICE FOR YOU.

I KNOW. I LIKED THE CAR.

DON'T YOU THINK IT'D BE NICE IF YOU TOLD HIM THAT?

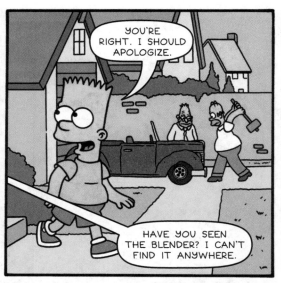

YOU'RE RIGHT. I SHOULD APOLOGIZE.

HAVE YOU SEEN THE BLENDER? I CAN'T FIND IT ANYWHERE.

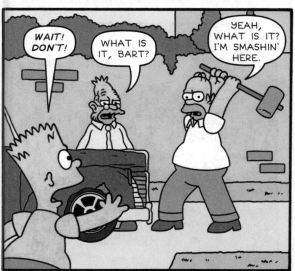

WAIT! DON'T!

WHAT IS IT, BART?

YEAH, WHAT IS IT? I'M SMASHIN' HERE.

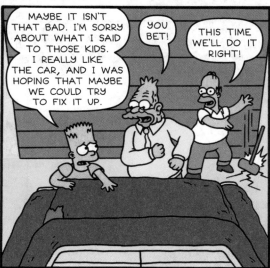

MAYBE IT ISN'T THAT BAD. I'M SORRY ABOUT WHAT I SAID TO THOSE KIDS. I REALLY LIKE THE CAR, AND I WAS HOPING THAT MAYBE WE COULD TRY TO FIX IT UP.

YOU BET!

THIS TIME WE'LL DO IT RIGHT!

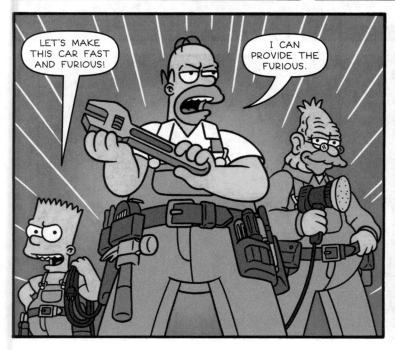

LET'S MAKE THIS CAR FAST AND FURIOUS!

I CAN PROVIDE THE FURIOUS.

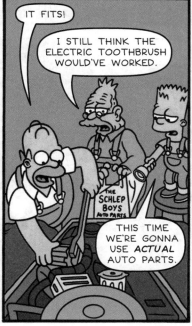

IT FITS!

I STILL THINK THE ELECTRIC TOOTHBRUSH WOULD'VE WORKED.

THE SCHLEP BOYS AUTO PARTS

THIS TIME WE'RE GONNA USE ACTUAL AUTO PARTS.

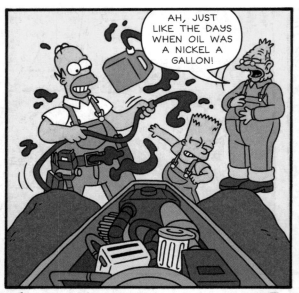

AH, JUST LIKE THE DAYS WHEN OIL WAS A NICKEL A GALLON!

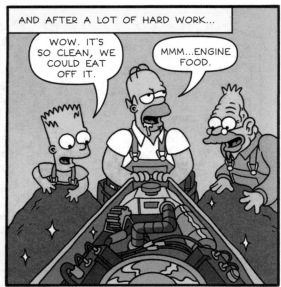

AND AFTER A LOT OF HARD WORK...

WOW. IT'S SO CLEAN, WE COULD EAT OFF IT.

MMM...ENGINE FOOD.

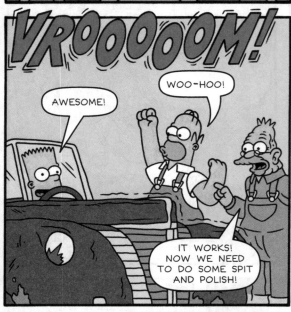

VROOOOOM!

AWESOME!

WOO-HOO!

IT WORKS! NOW WE NEED TO DO SOME SPIT AND POLISH!

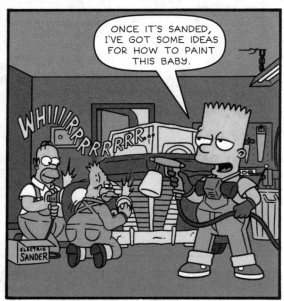

ONCE IT'S SANDED, I'VE GOT SOME IDEAS FOR HOW TO PAINT THIS BABY.

WHIIIIRRRRRRR...

ELECTRIC SANDER

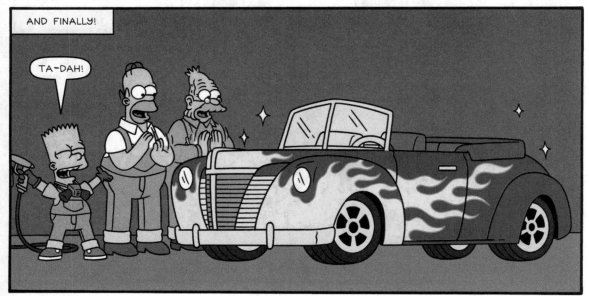

AND FINALLY!

TA-DAH!

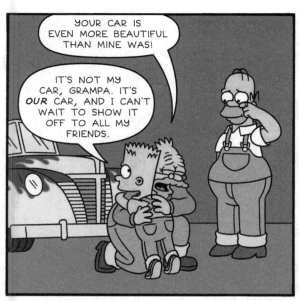

YOUR CAR IS EVEN MORE BEAUTIFUL THAN MINE WAS!

IT'S NOT MY CAR, GRAMPA. IT'S *OUR* CAR, AND I CAN'T WAIT TO SHOW IT OFF TO ALL MY FRIENDS.

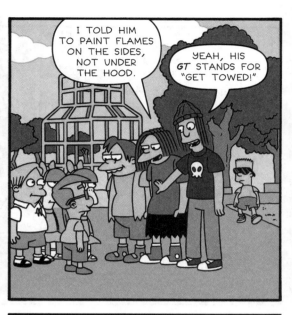

I TOLD HIM TO PAINT FLAMES ON THE SIDES, NOT UNDER THE HOOD.

YEAH, HIS *GT* STANDS FOR "GET TOWED!"

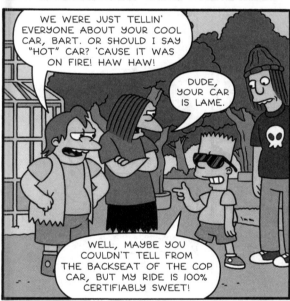

WE WERE JUST TELLIN' EVERYONE ABOUT YOUR COOL CAR, BART. OR SHOULD I SAY "HOT" CAR? 'CAUSE IT WAS ON FIRE! HAW HAW!

DUDE, YOUR CAR IS LAME.

WELL, MAYBE YOU COULDN'T TELL FROM THE BACKSEAT OF THE COP CAR, BUT MY RIDE IS 100% CERTIFIABLY SWEET!

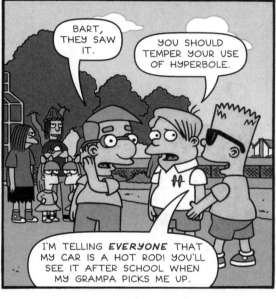

BART, THEY SAW IT.

YOU SHOULD TEMPER YOUR USE OF HYPERBOLE.

I'M TELLING *EVERYONE* THAT MY CAR IS A HOT ROD! YOU'LL SEE IT AFTER SCHOOL WHEN MY GRAMPA PICKS ME UP.

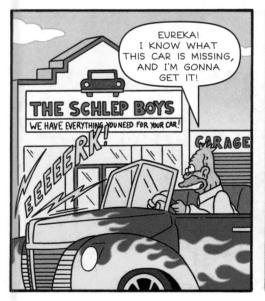

EUREKA! I KNOW WHAT THIS CAR IS MISSING, AND I'M GONNA GET IT!

THE SCHLEP BOYS
WE HAVE EVERYTHING YOU NEED FOR YOUR CAR!

GARAGE

EEEEERK!

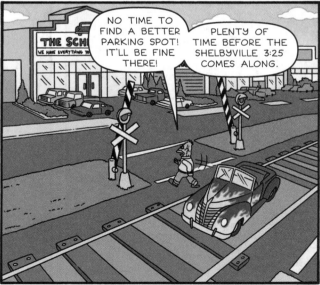

NO TIME TO FIND A BETTER PARKING SPOT! IT'LL BE FINE THERE!

PLENTY OF TIME BEFORE THE SHELBYVILLE 3:25 COMES ALONG.

THE SCHL
WE HAVE EVERYTHING YO

SEE, THIS RACCOON TAIL IS JUST LIKE THE ONE I HUNG FROM MY ANTENNA!
IT'S THE PERFECT FINISHING TOUCH TO MY GRANDSON'S CAR.
WHOOOO OOOOH EOOOOH!
WHAT'S THAT RUCKUS? IT'S SOUNDS LIKE A TRAIN.
THAT'S THE SHELBYVILLE 3:15.
SCHLEP BOYS
NOT **3:25**? UH-OH!
ERT! SMASH! CRACK! CHUG! BOOM! SHATTER!
SWEET RIDE, SIMPSON.
I SEE WHAT YOU MEANT. YOUR CAR IS 100% SOMETHING.
WE DON'T THINK YOU ROCK ANYMORE.
HAW HAW!
OH, GRAMPA.
CAN YOU GIVE **ME** A RIDE HOME?
THE CAR WAS NICE, BUT I REALLY DON'T NEED ONE YET.
YOU GOT THAT RIGHT. THIS IS ONE SWEET RIDE!
THE END

# MAGGIE'S CRIB

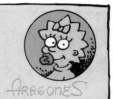

by ARAGONÉS

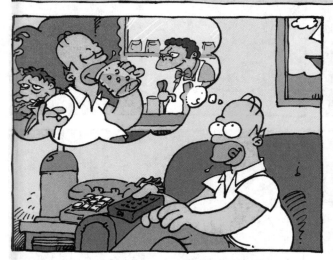

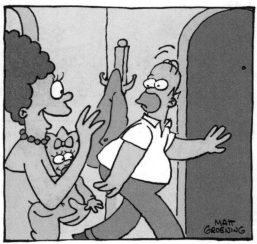

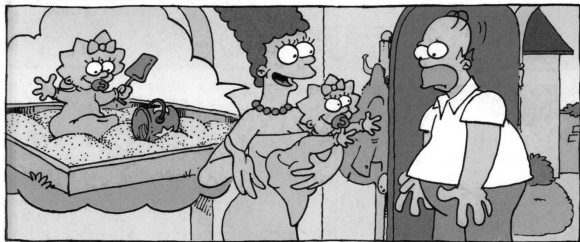

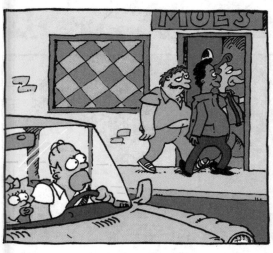

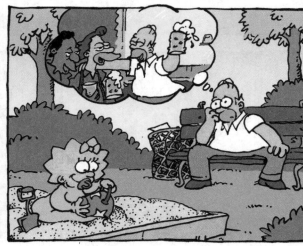

**SERGIO ARAGONÉS**
STORY & ART

**ART VILLANUEVA**
COLORS

**BILL MORRISON**
EDITOR

KEEP
CLEAN

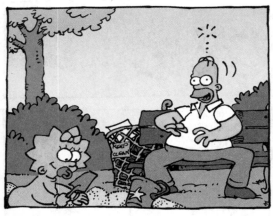

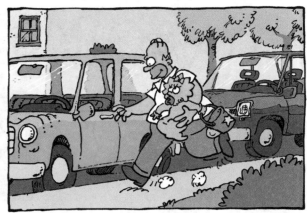

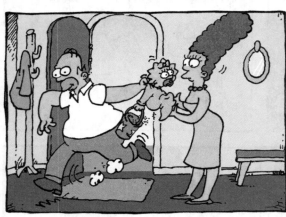

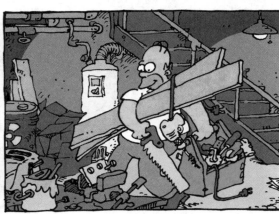

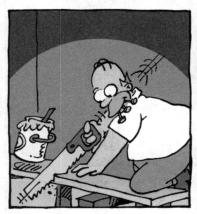

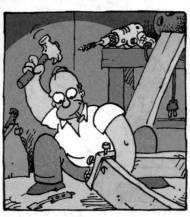

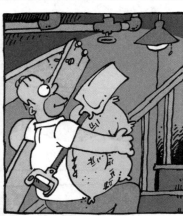

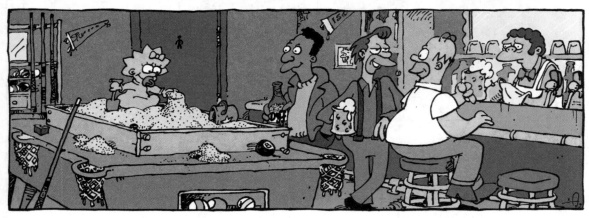

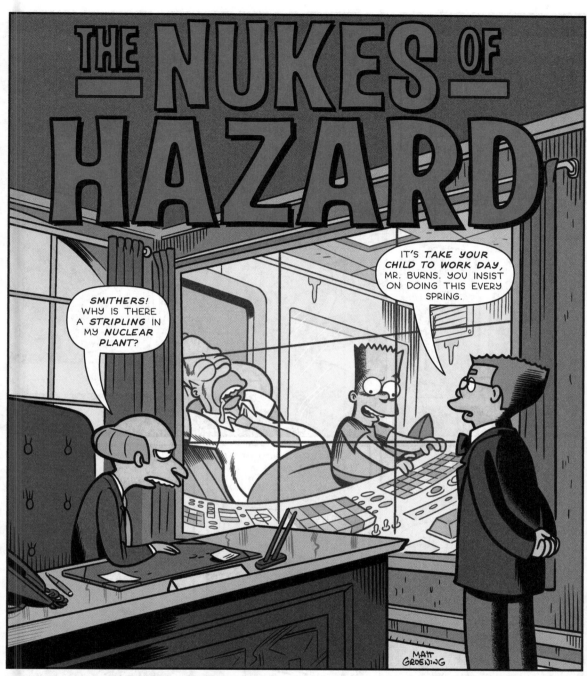

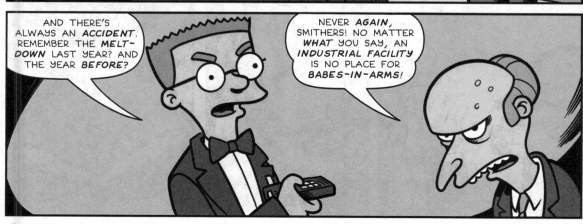

**TOM PEYER**
SCRIPT

**JOHN DELANEY**
PENCILS

**DAN DAVIS**
INKS

**ART VILLANUEVA**
COLORS

**KAREN BATES**
LETTERS

**BILL MORRISON**
EDITOR

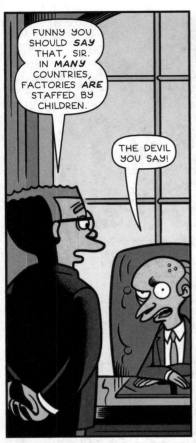

FUNNY YOU SHOULD *SAY* THAT, SIR. IN *MANY* COUNTRIES, FACTORIES *ARE* STAFFED BY CHILDREN.

THE DEVIL YOU SAY!

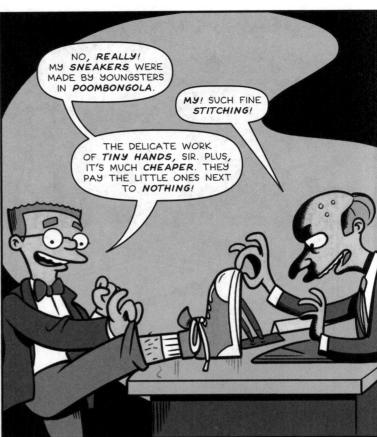

NO, *REALLY!* MY *SNEAKERS* WERE MADE BY YOUNGSTERS IN *POOMBONGOLA.*

*MY!* SUCH FINE *STITCHING!*

THE DELICATE WORK OF *TINY HANDS,* SIR. PLUS, IT'S MUCH *CHEAPER.* THEY PAY THE LITTLE ONES NEXT TO *NOTHING!*

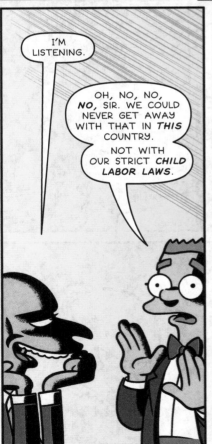

I'M LISTENING.

OH, NO, NO, *NO,* SIR. WE COULD NEVER GET AWAY WITH THAT IN *THIS* COUNTRY.

NOT WITH OUR STRICT *CHILD LABOR LAWS.*

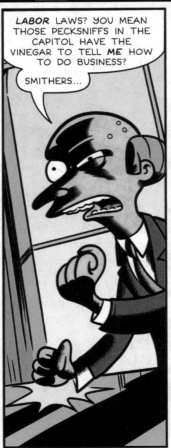

*LABOR* LAWS? YOU MEAN THOSE PECKSNIFFS IN THE CAPITOL HAVE THE VINEGAR TO TELL *ME* HOW TO DO BUSINESS?

SMITHERS...

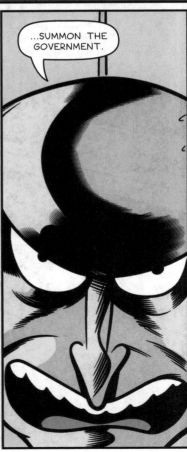

...SUMMON THE GOVERNMENT.

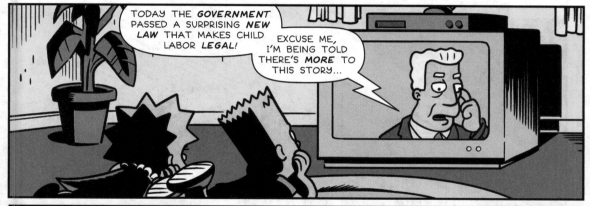

TODAY THE *GOVERNMENT* PASSED A SURPRISING *NEW* LAW THAT MAKES CHILD LABOR *LEGAL!*

EXCUSE ME, I'M BEING TOLD THERE'S *MORE* TO THIS STORY...

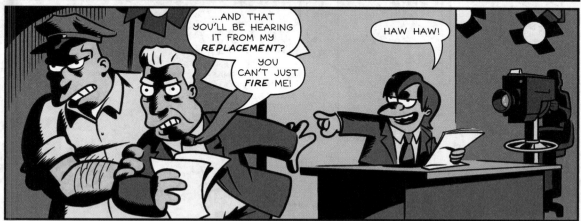

...AND THAT YOU'LL BE HEARING IT FROM MY *REPLACEMENT?* YOU CAN'T JUST *FIRE* ME!

HAW HAW!

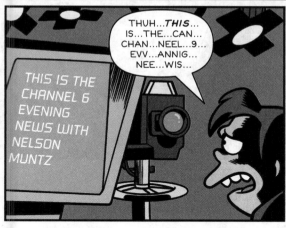

THUH...*THIS*...IS...THE...CAN...CHAN...NEEL...9...EVV...ANNIG...NEE...WIS...

THIS IS THE CHANNEL 6 EVENING NEWS WITH NELSON MUNTZ

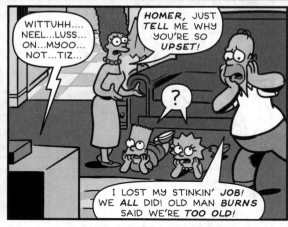

WITTUHH....NEEL...LUSS...ON...MYOO...NOT...TIZ...

*HOMER,* JUST *TELL* ME WHY YOU'RE SO *UPSET!*

?

I LOST MY STINKIN' *JOB!* WE *ALL* DID! OLD MAN *BURNS* SAID WE'RE *TOO* OLD!

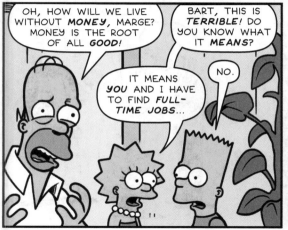

OH, HOW WILL WE LIVE WITHOUT *MONEY,* MARGE? MONEY IS THE ROOT OF ALL *GOOD!*

BART, THIS IS *TERRIBLE!* DO YOU KNOW WHAT IT *MEANS?*

IT MEANS *YOU* AND I HAVE TO FIND *FULL-TIME JOBS...*

NO.

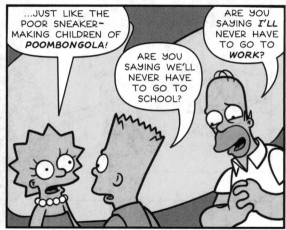

...JUST LIKE THE POOR SNEAKER-MAKING CHILDREN OF *POOMBONGOLA!*

ARE YOU SAYING *I'LL* NEVER HAVE TO GO TO *WORK?*

ARE YOU SAYING WE'LL NEVER HAVE TO GO TO SCHOOL?

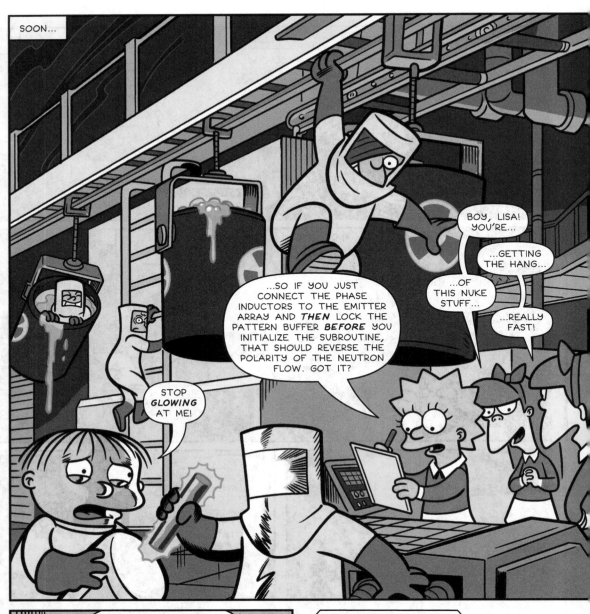

SOON...

BOY, LISA! YOU'RE...

...GETTING THE HANG...

...OF THIS NUKE STUFF...

...REALLY FAST!

...SO IF YOU JUST CONNECT THE PHASE INDUCTORS TO THE EMITTER ARRAY AND *THEN* LOCK THE PATTERN BUFFER *BEFORE* YOU INITIALIZE THE SUBROUTINE, THAT SHOULD REVERSE THE POLARITY OF THE NEUTRON FLOW. GOT IT?

STOP *GLOWING* AT ME!

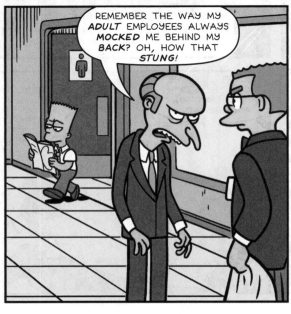

REMEMBER THE WAY MY *ADULT* EMPLOYEES ALWAYS *MOCKED* ME BEHIND MY *BACK*? OH, HOW THAT *STUNG*!

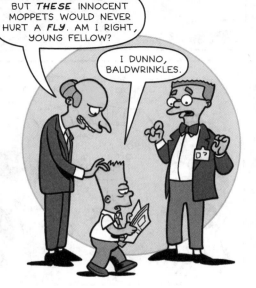

BUT *THESE* INNOCENT MOPPETS WOULD NEVER HURT A *FLY*. AM I RIGHT, YOUNG FELLOW?

I DUNNO, BALDWRINKLES.

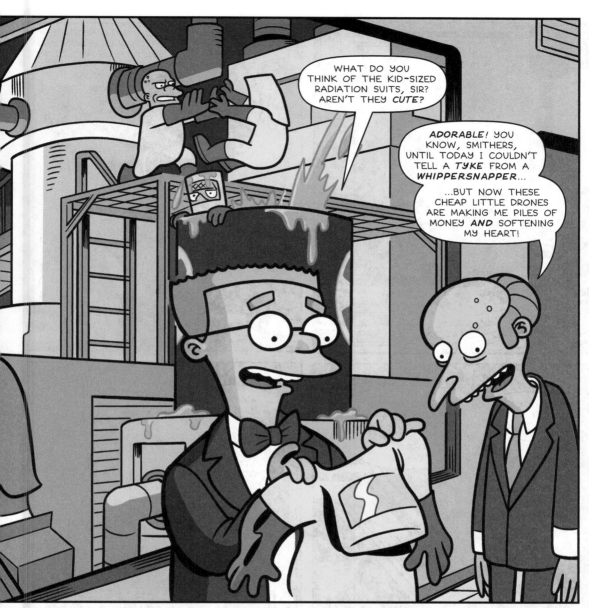

WHAT DO YOU THINK OF THE KID-SIZED RADIATION SUITS, SIR? AREN'T THEY *CUTE*?

*ADORABLE!* YOU KNOW, SMITHERS, UNTIL TODAY I COULDN'T TELL A *TYKE* FROM A *WHIPPERSNAPPER*...

...BUT NOW THESE CHEAP LITTLE DRONES ARE MAKING ME PILES OF MONEY *AND* SOFTENING MY HEART!

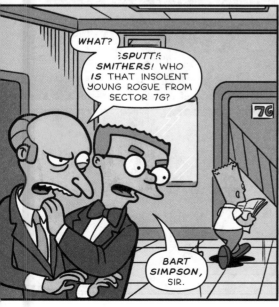

*WHAT?*

≣SPUTT!≣ *SMITHERS!* WHO *IS* THAT INSOLENT YOUNG ROGUE FROM SECTOR 7G?

BART SIMPSON, SIR.

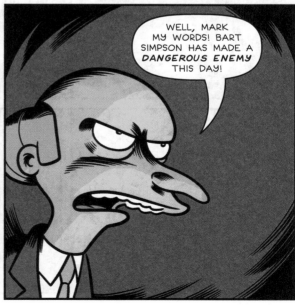

WELL, MARK MY WORDS! BART SIMPSON HAS MADE A *DANGEROUS ENEMY* THIS DAY!

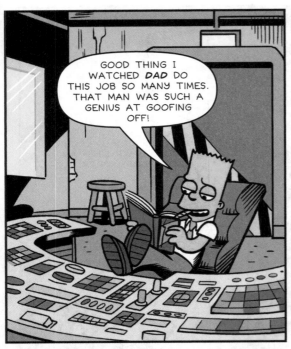

GOOD THING I WATCHED *DAD* DO THIS JOB SO MANY TIMES. THAT MAN WAS SUCH A GENIUS AT GOOFING OFF!

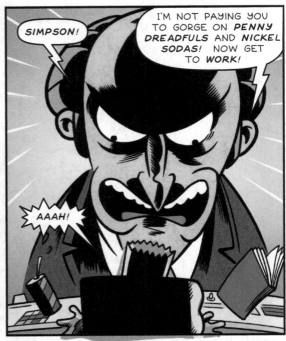

SIMPSON!

I'M NOT PAYING YOU TO GORGE ON *PENNY DREADFULS* AND *NICKEL SODAS*! NOW GET TO *WORK*!

AAAH!

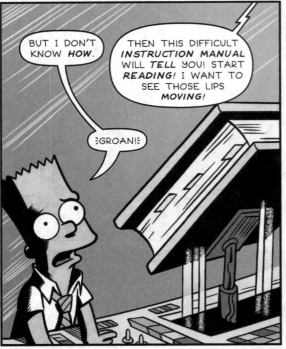

BUT I DON'T KNOW *HOW*.

THEN THIS DIFFICULT *INSTRUCTION MANUAL* WILL *TELL* YOU! START *READING*! I WANT TO SEE THOSE LIPS *MOVING*!

≷GROAN!≷

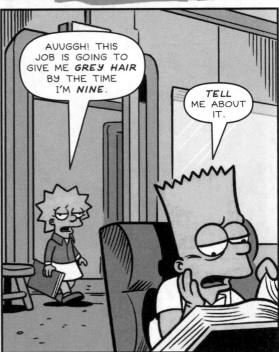

AUUGGH! THIS JOB IS GOING TO GIVE ME *GREY HAIR* BY THE TIME I'M *NINE*.

*TELL* ME ABOUT IT.

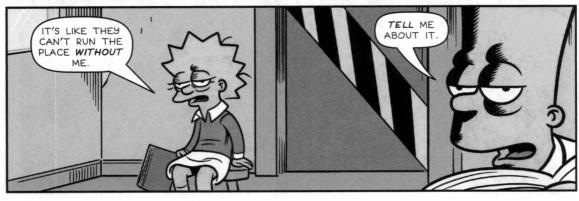

IT'S LIKE THEY CAN'T RUN THE PLACE *WITHOUT* ME.

*TELL* ME ABOUT IT.

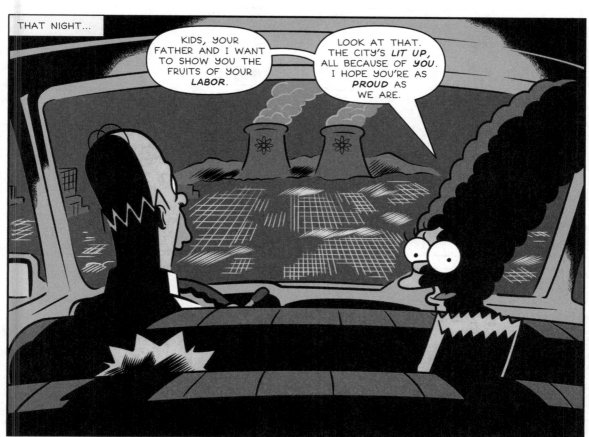

KIDS, YOUR FATHER AND I WANT TO SHOW YOU THE FRUITS OF YOUR *LABOR*.

LOOK AT THAT. THE CITY'S *LIT UP*, ALL BECAUSE OF *YOU*. I HOPE YOU'RE AS *PROUD* AS WE ARE.

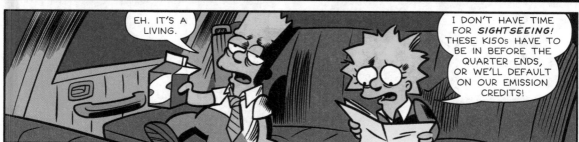

EH. IT'S A LIVING.

I DON'T HAVE TIME FOR *SIGHTSEEING!* THESE K150s HAVE TO BE IN BEFORE THE QUARTER ENDS, OR WE'LL DEFAULT ON OUR EMISSION CREDITS!

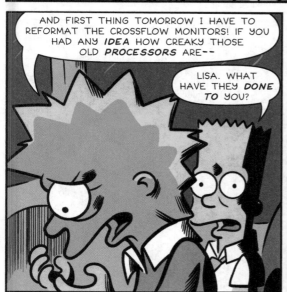

AND FIRST THING TOMORROW I HAVE TO REFORMAT THE CROSSFLOW MONITORS! IF YOU HAD ANY *IDEA* HOW CREAKY THOSE OLD *PROCESSORS* ARE--

LISA. WHAT HAVE THEY *DONE TO* YOU?

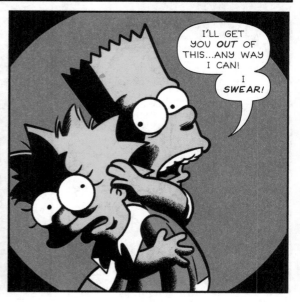

I'LL GET YOU *OUT* OF THIS...ANY WAY I CAN! I *SWEAR!*

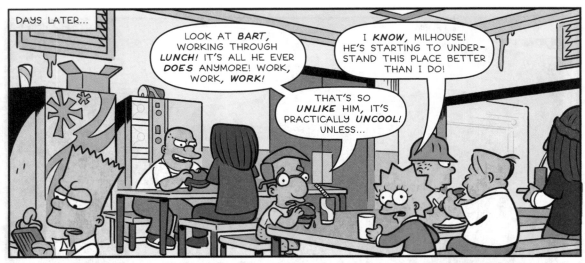

DAYS LATER...

LOOK AT *BART*, WORKING THROUGH *LUNCH*! IT'S ALL HE EVER *DOES* ANYMORE! WORK, WORK, *WORK*!

I *KNOW*, MILHOUSE! HE'S STARTING TO UNDER-STAND THIS PLACE BETTER THAN I DO!

THAT'S SO *UNLIKE* HIM, IT'S PRACTICALLY *UNCOOL*! UNLESS...

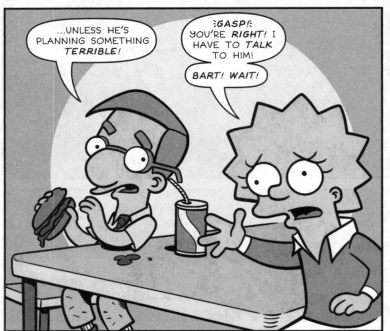

...UNLESS HE'S PLANNING SOMETHING *TERRIBLE*!

⁝GASP!⁝ YOU'RE *RIGHT*! I HAVE TO *TALK* TO HIM!

BART! WAIT!

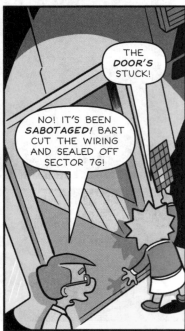

THE DOOR'S STUCK!

NO! IT'S BEEN *SABOTAGED*! BART CUT THE WIRING AND SEALED OFF SECTOR 7G!

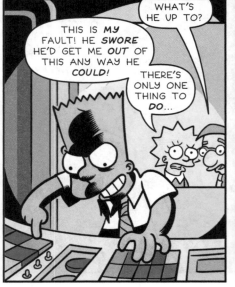

WHAT'S HE UP TO?

THIS IS *MY* FAULT! HE *SWORE* HE'D GET ME *OUT* OF THIS ANY WAY HE *COULD*!

THERE'S ONLY ONE THING TO *DO*...

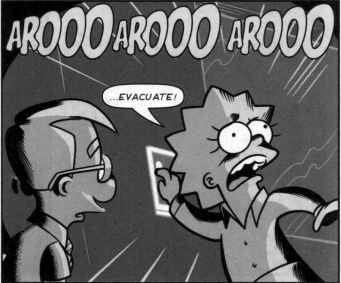

AROOO AROOO AROOO

...EVACUATE!

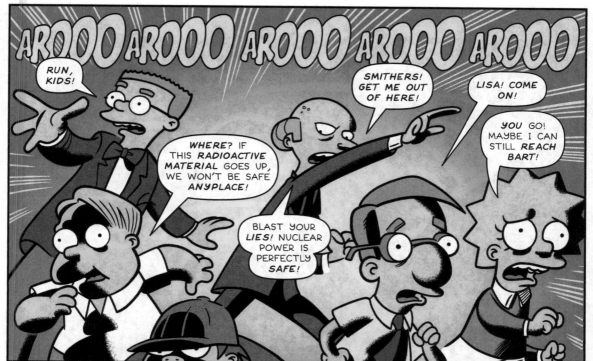

AROOO AROOO AROOO AROOO AROOO

RUN, KIDS!

WHERE? IF THIS *RADIOACTIVE MATERIAL* GOES UP, WE WON'T BE SAFE *ANYPLACE!*

SMITHERS! GET ME OUT OF HERE!

LISA! COME ON!

YOU GO! MAYBE I CAN STILL *REACH* BART!

BLAST YOUR *LIES!* NUCLEAR POWER IS PERFECTLY *SAFE!*

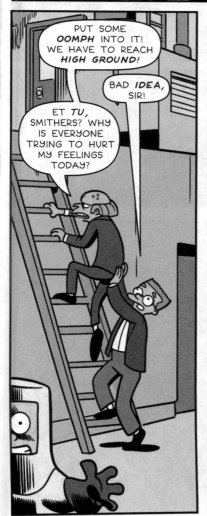

PUT SOME *OOMPH* INTO IT! WE HAVE TO REACH *HIGH GROUND!*

BAD *IDEA,* SIR!

ET *TU,* SMITHERS? WHY IS EVERYONE TRYING TO HURT MY FEELINGS TODAY?

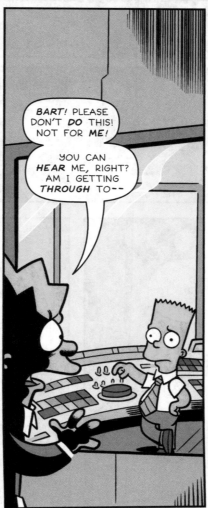

BART! PLEASE DON'T *DO* THIS! NOT FOR *ME!*

YOU CAN *HEAR* ME, RIGHT? AM I GETTING *THROUGH* TO--

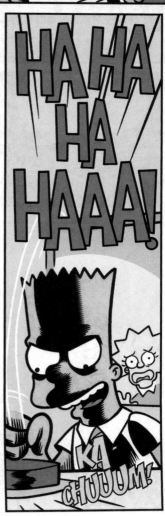

HA HA HA HAAA!

KA CHUUUM!

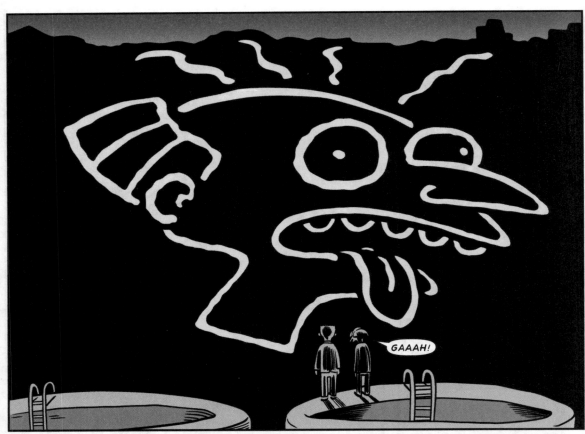

GAAAH!

SMITHERS, DO YOU REMEMBER HOW THE ADULTS USED TO MOCK ME *BEHIND* MY BACK?

YES, SIR.

CAN WE HAVE THAT AGAIN?

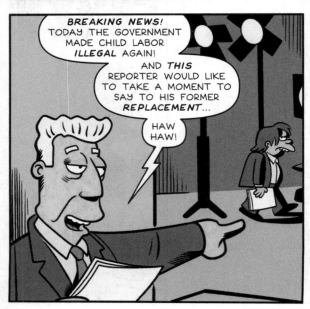

*BREAKING NEWS!* TODAY THE GOVERNMENT MADE CHILD LABOR *ILLEGAL* AGAIN!

AND *THIS* REPORTER WOULD LIKE TO TAKE A MOMENT TO SAY TO HIS FORMER *REPLACEMENT*...

HAW HAW!

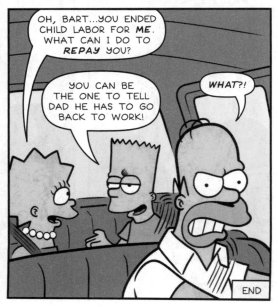

OH, BART...YOU ENDED CHILD LABOR FOR *ME*. WHAT CAN I DO TO *REPAY* YOU?

YOU CAN BE THE ONE TO TELL DAD HE HAS TO GO BACK TO WORK!

*WHAT*?!

END